Saint Dominic

YOUR NAME—YOUR SAINT

YOUR NAME—YOUR SAINT SERIES

SAINT AGNES
By Louise André-Delastre

SAINT NICHOLAS
By Jeanne Ancelet-Hustache

SAINT MARTIN
By Edith Delamare

SAINT VINCENT DE PAUL
By Louis Chaigne

SAINT JEROME
By Regina and Madeleine Pernoud

SAINT BENEDICT
By Marie de Miserey

SAINT DOMINIC
By Marie-Dominique Poinsenet

SAINT DOMINIC

BY

Marie-Dominique Poinsenet

TRANSLATED BY

John Chapin

THE MACMILLAN COMPANY

NEW YORK

Nihil obstat
> James A. Reynolds
> CENSOR LIBRORUM

Imprimatur
> ✠ Francis Cardinal Spellman
> ARCHBISHOP OF NEW YORK

August 17, 1962

The nihil obstat and imprimatur are official declarations that a book or pamphlet is free of doctrinal or moral error. No implication is contained therein that those who have granted the nihil obstat and imprimatur agree with the contents, opinions or statements expressed.

First Printing

The Macmillan Company, New York
Collier-Macmillan Canada Ltd., Galt, Ontario
Divisions of The Crowell-Collier Publishing Company

Printed in the United States of America

Library of Congress catalog card number: 63-8397

Contents

Contents

Foreword

The life of St. Dominic was both distorted and en-
cumbered in the period between the thirteenth and
sixteenth centuries by a host of apocryphal legends,
which we owe to the pens of various chroniclers, whose
good intentions, laudable though the latter may have
been, are no compensation for the bad taste of these
authors, or, what is even more distressing, for their
almost complete lack of any historical sense. Ever since
the biography by Père Lacordaire made its appearance,
a serious effort has been under way to get back to the
authentic sources for the life of the Father of the Order

of Preachers and to isolate the true story from the mass of edifying material surrounding it, which has served to distort the real image. The latter is much more attractive and inspiring when viewed in its primitive, simple, unadorned state.

The two volumes of Père M. H. Vicaire, O.P., published by Editions du Cerf in 1957 and entitled *Histoire de saint Dominique,* are regarded as authoritative on this subject. No biographer of the Saint of Caleruega can afford, henceforth, to ignore this important work, the result of long labor and painstaking research, which goes into the question of the origins of the Order of Preachers and the history of its founder more thoroughly and satisfactorily than any other work.

May I take this opportunity, therefore, to express my heartfelt thanks to the Reverend Father Vicaire for the kind permission given the author of the following modest pages to draw on the great wealth of information contained in the above-mentioned work.

M. D. P.

Saint Dominic

1

In a Deserted Land

"Dominice, ego te baptizo, in nomine Patris et Filii et Spiritus Sancti." The saving waters flowed over the brow of a son of Caleruega. The Church was blessed with one more member. The good news was announced to the entire village by the bells of the little Romanesque parish church. The children playing in the streets ran shouting to the village square with its fountain in order to be the first to catch a glimpse of the third son of Juana de Aza and Felix de Guzman, who had just been born to them in the year of grace 1171.[1] His mother Juana had insisted that he be named Dominic, so that he would be under the powerful protection of St. Dominic of Silos, the famous Benedictine abbot who was honored by every Castilian. Like all other mothers in that part of the world, Juana had paid a visit to the abbey which was only a few miles distant from Caleruega, while waiting for the birth of her son. She had knelt at the foot of the altar, adorned with the heavy chains and cumbersome iron rings offered to the saint by prisoners, as a sign of gratitude, on their release from terrible Moorish captivity.

As abbot of Silos, Dominic had also been under the protection of an earlier Dominic. In addition to this Dominic, we also find several other Dominics mentioned in the Martyrology, including St. Dominic, an African martyr, and St. Dominica, a virgin, who was martyred in Campania under the emperor Diocletian. Much nearer to our own time there would also be a St. Dominic Savio, the pupil of Don Bosco, who died at the age of fifteen.

"The saints provide us with our Christian names," explains Louis Lavelle;[2] "this not only helps to differentiate them from each other, but to make them more real to us, and places each one of us under their patronage so that, in a certain sense, we are taking them for our model. . . . Because the nature of man is so infinitely various and can never be fully probed, the saints too differ profoundly from each other."

Some have maintained that the name of Dominic (*Dominicus, Dominica*) is an adjective deriving from

2

the Latin word *Dominus* and means a man (or woman) "belonging to the Lord." According to a late etymology the word *Dominicani*, applied to the spiritual sons of Dominic of Caleruega, is derived from the play on words, *Domini canes*. Whether or not this is so, it is certain that medieval man, ever prone to look for a symbolical meaning in things, was fond of regarding the Preachers as the "hounds of God," because they had been entrusted by the Church with the task of bringing the wandering sheep back to the fold. There can be no doubt also that this allegorical way of looking at things gave rise to the story of the "dream" of Juana de Aza. Before the birth of Dominic, his mother is supposed to have had a vision of the child she was carrying racing across the world in the form of a little black and white dog, which was carrying a flaming torch in its teeth. The same story, it is true, identical in almost all details, was told of Blessed Aleth, the mother of St. Bernard of Clairvaux. How much legend and how much historical truth are there in miraculous stories of this kind? It is difficult to say. The symbolism, in any case, was readily apparent and has been consecrated by art over the centuries. The fresco of Andrea da Firenze in the chapel of the Spaniards in Florence is perhaps one of the most famous of these representations.

Neither the country nor the age makes the man. But every man bears the mark of his country and his age. The saints, too, are subject to this general rule, because they are also men.

Wandering across the high plateau country of Old Castile, with its poor stony soil and its harsh, fierce beauty, we get a better insight into the soul of the Father of the Friars Preachers than by paying heed to the numerous apocryphal legends which over the centuries have obscured the sharp image of a life at once both varied and simple, under the pretext of rendering it more edifying. We find traces of him in the tiny *pueblo* of Caleruega. Viewed from a distance, the small houses of red clay seem to be one with the soil itself and are not very different from those in existence at the time when Philip Augustus was preparing to depart for the Third Crusade. The Romanesque church, a portion of which is now incorporated in a later edifice, had then just been built. Mules, cows, and sheep drank from the fountain in the village square in those days just as they do today. The only remains of the modest fortified castle where Dominic was born are a square tower constructed of solid rock—the *torreon*. For his father was the master (*dominus*)— we can hardly say lord—of a few peasant families who had clustered under the protecting walls of the Guzman residence toward the beginning of the twelfth century.

On the east, towering above the village, is a great rock called *la peña de San Jorge*. This dominates the arid plateau, swept in turn by gusts of wind, rain, and snow throughout two-thirds of the year. During the summer months the countryside is parched by the unmerciful rays of the sun. The plateau is about 2,800 feet above sea level at this particular point, while *San Jorge* itself stands exactly 3,280 feet high. There are few if any trees, some clusters of black pine, but none nearer than a mile or two away.

As a child Dominic doubtless climbed the *peña* with his brothers and fellow playmates in the village, for he lived at Caleruega until he was seven. It was there that his eyes first discovered the world in which he was to live. Day after day, as a very young child, these eyes became accustomed to the sight of the harsh barrenness of his native soil, the unrelieved vastness of the red plateau stretching as far as the wall of the Sierra Guadarrama, which he could just discern in the distance. The impression made on men by this *deznudez* or denuded landscape was not of a kind to imprison the heart, but to turn the soul instinctively toward the infinite.

"In terra deserta, et invia et inaquosa . . .

"In a desert land, and where there is no way, and no water: so in the sanctuary have I come before thee, to see thy power and thy glory. . . ."

We cannot help thinking of this verse of Psalm 62 as we contemplate the contours of this land. We seem to be discovering its meaning for the first time, while at the same time another biblical passage comes to mind, the reply, it has been called, to the prayer of the psalmist. I refer to the words of the Canticle of Canticles:

"Introduxit me rex in cellam vinariam, ordinavit in me caritatem."

"He [the king] brought me into his cellar of wine, he set in order charity in me."

For as a matter of fact, *bodegas* have been hewn out of the limestone walls of the *Peña de San Jorge* as well as the nearby cliffs, to serve as primitive wine cellars, so that the wine can be stored right in the vineyard itself, while, on the slopes farther down, shepherds, wearing the ancient garb of their calling, "lead their flocks to pasture" across the sparse pasture lands of the *vega*.

So when little Dominic went to Gumiel de Izan, to the house of his uncle the archpriest, to begin his schooling, he took with him a twofold love which would explain the whole course of his life: a love of God and a love of men in God, as well as the desire to deprive oneself of everything which, being merely human, is not good enough for a heart created for the infinite, since it has been created for God.

While Dominic was a son of Caleruega, he was also, at the same time, a son of the *reconquistadores*. The age when he was born and grew up was a troubled one. Spain was still struggling, inch by inch, both to regain its land and its independence from the

Moors, and to protect its faith. The Moors still occupied more than a third of the peninsula, and Toledo was then the scene of numerous bloody battles. Many Christians were still being held in chains beyond the Tagus, or had renounced their faith! The Muslims had strongholds almost at the mouth of the Ebro. A new raid was possible at any time. The thick walls of the small castle of Caleruega reminded the three boys every night when they went to sleep that their country was not yet fully at peace.

Spain was going through a troubled period. But was not all of Christendom itself in a similar deplorable condition? The Church was tottering on its foundations, suffering from the twin evils of too much temporal wealth and the ignorance of the clergy, which were eating away at its entrails like a cancer. This distressing state of affairs inspired the famous legend of the "Dream of Innocent III," which would be graphically portrayed by the two famous Franciscan and Dominican painters, Giotto and Fra Angelico.

Dominic was as yet not conscious of things of this kind. But God was nevertheless leading him, unconsciously, toward his true destiny.

It is probable that when the young child arrived at Gumiel de Izan, where he took up residence in the house of his uncle the archpriest, he found companions of his own age, in accordance with the custom of the time. Learning Latin in those days was no easy business! Every class worthy of the name was dominated by the

7

inexorable rule of the rod and the switch. We can be quite certain that during the few years which Dominic was obliged to spend in the village of Gumiel he received a sound training and was subject to stern discipline. Studies of this nature, at such an early age, meant moreover that the young boy was being destined for the clergy. The young clerics of those days learned to read from the Psalter and were taught how to sing the Gregorian melodies of the Latin responses and hymns from the parchment pages of the huge folio antiphonaries open on the lectern.

Students only went on to a higher school at the age of fourteen or fifteen. About the year 1185, therefore, Dominic left Gumiel de Izan to go to Palencia, where he remained for eight or perhaps ten years. The school at Palencia had not as yet been designated a university. It would receive this coveted honor only in 1208, when it became the first school in Spain to be called a university. The course of studies, however, must have consisted of the seven liberal arts of the *Trivium* and *Quadrivium* which formed the backbone of instruction in medieval universities: grammar, dialectics, rhetoric, arithmetic, music, geometry, and astronomy.

The atmosphere of the town, too, was typical of any place where students were to be found, being noted for its more or less easygoing ways, its boisterous night life, and occasionally riots, which were the terror of the peaceloving citizens. The exuberant students appeared, at times, to be more interested in tormenting the townsmen than in attending classes.

Now it was precisely his attitude toward these things that was most revealing about the true nature of Dominic. Without any pressure being brought to bear on him, he gave clear signs, from the first, of belonging to the category of quiet, plodding students. In this respect he was simply following the twofold dictate of his mind and his heart. Studies attracted him, not because they were good in themselves, but because he saw them as a human means for arriving at a closer knowledge of the truth as revealed in the sacred science of the Scriptures. Moreover his whole nature was opposed to any kind of cheap bargaining, or compromise, in the matter of a complete gift of himself which he had resolved to make, entirely voluntarily, by becoming a priest of the Lord.

Jordan of Saxony is our authority for the following interesting observation about Dominic, the truth of which can hardly be doubted: "When he felt that he had derived enough from the profane sciences, he ceased to devote himself to them any more, out of fear, as it were, that he might be wasting the little time that remained to him here on earth for the sake of insufficient rewards. . . . He at once took up the study of sacred theology and began to devote himself wholeheartedly to the Sacred Scriptures. . . . Four years were devoted to the study of theology. . . . He was tireless when it was a question of study."

As soon as he was old enough to have his own room for study he proceeded to hire one, attracted by the prospect of leading a life of silence and solitude, which would then become possible. He lived very simply, devoting at least a part of each night to study. His manuscripts were his only prized possessions. The text of the Bible, for example, which he had copied with his own hand on parchment, amounted to a small fortune in itself. But when he had annotated it with the lectures of his teachers and thus came into possession of a veritable series of commentaries, it became an indispensable tool for his work and a treasure so priceless that it could simply not be evaluated in terms of money. Dominic was well aware of all this. And it would have been perfectly fitting for a student and lover of learning to feel attached to his books as real treasures. No one would have found fault with this. But the young theologian of Palencia was more than a humanist, a mere lover of learning—he was a man, a human being.

The truth of this statement is well attested by a certain incident for which there is reliable historical evidence.

One year all Spain was visited by one of those terrible famines which periodically plagued the province where Dominic lived. Both the extreme aridity of the Castilian plateau and the lack of streams seem to confirm the truth of the story, as told by his biographers. Owing to a twofold struggle then being waged, between the Christian princes of Castile and Leon in the north, and between the kingdoms of Cordova and Granada in the south, the people were reduced to the direst straits and were dying from hunger both in the towns and in the countryside. And, as always, the shamefulness of those who were prepared to profit from black market operations at such times knew no limits. It seems that the students at Palencia had sufficient supplies to tide them over. One of them, however, found himself unable to adopt a complaisant attitude toward the sufferings of others.

"Moved by the misery of the poor, Dominic resolved, at one and the same time, to heed the evangelical counsels and relieve the misery of the dying poor, to the extent of his ability. With this thought in mind, he proceeded to sell the books that he had and all his valuable possessions. Thus providing himself with a small fund for alms, that is, something to hand out to the poor each day in the way of food, he took what he had and gave it to the poor."

When one of his colleagues professed surprise and shock that he was willing to part with his maunscripts, Dominic simply said to him: "I cannot study from dead skins, when men are dying from hunger." Soon the news of what he had done got abroad. The surprise of some then turned to admiration. Good, like evil, can be contagious. Certain of the theologians, both students and what was even more remarkable, a number of the masters, "suddenly becoming aware of their own laxness and avarice compared to the generosity of this young man, and began to hand out considerable alms from that moment."

11

A fact of this kind was too unusual to escape the attention of contemporaries. What the young cleric of Palencia had done was soon talked about not only in the town but throughout the province. Doubtless the news also reached the ears of the bishop of Osma, who was looking for suitable clerics to be ordained to the higher orders in his diocese.

It was not difficult to win Dominic over. The latter was well aware that some clerics were attracted to the priesthood by nothing more than the human desire to possess a benefice. He was fully aware, also, that to some of the clergy the burdens of celibacy and poverty seemed too great to be borne. But for him these things were only one more reason why he was so eager to lead a truly evangelical life. The life of the canons of Osma was the one which most closely corresponded to these aspirations.

We must not imagine that the words *chapter* or *canon* had the same meaning for Dominic as they do for us today. The Chapter of Osma lived according to the Rule of St. Augustine. In order that the priests of his episcopal see might live more in conformity with their calling, the saintly bishop of Hippo had worked out a form of canonical life for them—the word *canon* means one subject to a rule—closely modeled on that of monks, so far as observances, discipline, and mortifications were concerned. The canonical rule meant that the individual was bound to live in a community and to recite the divine office in choir as part of his profession as a *canon regular*. What distinguished the latter from the monk most of all was his devotion to study rather than to manual labor. Hence, strange as it may seem, when the canonical way of life was observed most perfectly, it was more contemplative than the monastic way observed in the monasteries. Canons regular were bound to devote themselves to only one specifically practical activity, namely, the duties inherent in the apostolic mission of the priesthood, that is, the celebration of mass for the faithful, the administration of the sacraments, and preaching. However, they were normally called upon to perform these pastoral services only in the cathedral city itself. It was only rarely that they could do so elsewhere in the diocese, because the primary function of a canon was to see that the divine praise of the choral office was maintained day and night in the cathedral church.

The contemplative life of canons regular, however, was not of a kind which separated the chapter from the mass of the faithful, in the way that the anchorites were separated by their desert, or the monks by the walls of their monastery. It was in the cathedral choir and before all the people that the canons fulfilled their daily mission of bearing witness that they were "men consecrated to God."

Therefore when Dominic donned the white woolen tunic and black mantle and hood of the canons of Osma and took his place officially among the twelve canons of the chapter, he felt certain that he had found his true vocation. His profession and ordination as a priest must have seemed to be a kind of final seal determining the future course of his life, which, he thought, was destined to follow a well known pattern. It does not appear that he ever experienced anything that can be described as an inner spiritual struggle. There was merely a call and a response. His response, moreover, was not marked by any kind of bargaining but was made in absolute fidelity to the will of God, a trait characteristic of him throughout his life.

Dominic was so fitted for the life of a canon of Osma that he rose to be subprior before he had reached the age of thirty. A gifted nature as well as a deep sense of the spiritual, which could readily be observed in his whole demeanor although he himself was unaware of it, soon won him the esteem of all. Someday, no doubt, he would be destined for a more burdensome office, perhaps that of the episcopate.

This is what was in the minds of others, at any rate. But Dominic himself gave no thought to such matters: God was quite enough for him. There was nothing selfish or self-centered about his nature, for there is nothing which makes men more aware of others than the presence of God. The practical charity that induced the student of Palencia to sacrifice his valuable manuscripts on behalf of the hungry as the most natural thing in the world did not fade from the heart of the subprior of Osma. Far from it, it tended rather to grow and deepen, in proportion to the growth and depth of his sense of union with God. The following passage from Jordan of Saxony is instructive, in this regard, and needs no further commentary:

"God gave him the special grace of praying for sinners, the poor, and the afflicted. He bore their misfortunes in the secret recesses of his mercy, and the tears which flowed from his eyes revealed the intensity of the pity for them which burned in his heart. It was not unusual for him to spend the whole night in prayer. Behind closed doors, he prayed to his Father. While praying, he sometimes gave vent to the anguish felt in his heart by crying out or uttering words. Sometimes he could not restrain himself and his impassioned words could clearly be heard through the floor. One of his most frequent and persistent petitions to God was that He would give him real and efficacious love, so that he could devote himself wholeheartedly to the salvation of his fellowmen, for it seemed to him that he would only become a true member of Christ Himself when he could devote himself wholeheartedly to the winning of souls, as his Lord Jesus, the Saviour of all mankind, had consecrated Himself to the salvation of men." Though he burned with an inner fire, Dominic had as yet no desire to leave Osma, for he believed that it was his destined lot to remain there. He did not long for a broader field in which to exercise his ministry. He was nor anxious—at least with human anxiousness— to embark on the conquest of the world, even if the latter were to be solely for the glory of God. He merely begged, with equal insistence and confidence, for a single grace: "a real and efficacious love for the salvation of souls."

And there can be no doubt that this prayer reveals the extent to which Dominic had arrived at union with God. Such an ardent desire for the salvation of men is a sign both of an awareness of the divine transcendence and of the sin of men, which only the Holy Spirit can implant in the heart of man. It marked a beginning, if not yet a full realization, of the identification of himself with Christ, to which St. Paul referred when he said: "It is now no longer I that live, but Christ lives in me,"[5] that is, Christ with His infinite desire for the redemption of all mankind. As a matter of fact, by leading a life of silence, prayer, and renunciation in the cloister of Osma, Dominic was daily identifying himself more and more with Christ.

The world might choose to regard such a life as useless. Nevertheless, in it a tremendous impulse toward activity was latent. The latter would soon burst forth, with such intensity and grandeur, as to astound the world. God is pleased to do great things by means of one of His servants, but He Himself prepares the way in secret. The apostolate is not a human but a divine mission, which requires of man a complete denial of self and above all a flexibility, so that he will expose himself without reserve to the impulses of the Holy Spirit.

2

The Challenge of Albigensianism

The year 1203 marked the beginning of the second phase of the great adventure of the life of Dominic of Caleruega.

Alfonso XIII, king of Castile, was anxious to cement the ties between his kingdom and that of Denmark, and contemplated the marriage of his son, the Infante Ferdinand, to a princess of the distant "Marches of Dacia." As a suitable ambassador for such a delicate mission, his choice fell on a prelate of his own realm, Don Diego of Acebes, Bishop of Osma. The necessary escort for such an important journey was soon provided. The embassy set out in the month of May, 1203, and was soon crossing the Pyrenees. Accompanying the bishop of Osma as his personal "socius" was the lord Dominic, subprior of the chapter of Osma.

As soon as the little band had crossed the mountains, they realized that they were among heretics. They were well aware, of course, of the ravages in southern France caused by the Albigensian heresy. But it was one thing to know the fact and quite another to behold it with their own eyes. The Waldensians and especially the Cathari greeted the embassy of Alfonso XIII with looks of suspicion, impertinent challenges, or even taunts. Many Christians of the countryside and towns had been caught in the toils of the new error. Many of the local barons also were now flouting the laws observed throughout the rest of Christendom and were even permitting promoters of the heresy to live in impunity on their lands, or were going so far as actually to support them. The Cathari had seduced the common people by the austerity of their morals, whether pretended or real, as well as by the insidiousness and naïveté of their arguments. They were very adept at making themselves indispensable to the nobles. Their doctrine perhaps could not withstand a serious philosophical refutation. But neither the bishops, who had so many other things to occupy their time, nor the clergy, who had not been trained for a ministry of this kind, had been sufficiently alert to the

18

dangers of the situation. The preachers of the sect, most of whom belonged to the category of the *perfect,* had been very successful in adding to the number of *believers,* as a result of an intensive campaign of proselytism. Was it not perfectly natural to expect that people who were always prone to idle chatter and argumentation would be attracted by the persuasive voice of the novel doctrine? Especially when the latter seemed to be offering them a simple explanation of the age-old problem faced by men at all times and everywhere—the problem of evil and suffering.

Harking back to the old dualism of the Manichaeans, which had experienced a revival in Armenia and Bulgaria in the eighth and tenth centuries, the Cathari maintained that there were in fact two Gods. The God of the Gospel was the good God, the creator of the spiritual world only. The God of the Old Testament, on the other hand, the God of evil, was responsible for the creation of the material world, which was therefore evil. This doctrine, of course, undermined the very foundations of the Catholic faith. There was no Incarnation of the Son of God: Christ, whose divine Sonship the heretics denied, had only appeared to take on a human body, and could not have suffered. Consequently there could also be no resurrection of the flesh, for matter is evil, as well as no act of procreation, the fruit of marriage. Death was the great deliverance, because, by freeing the soul from the body, it restored the soul to the world of the angels. There was no hell or purgatory, of course. The *perfect* were regarded as living in a state of absolute purity. Those who were still only *believers* were destined to achieve their purification, if unrealized at the time of death, through a series of reincarnations in a future life. Thus the ancient oriental myth of metempsychosis was used in appealing to the imagination of weary and frustrated souls, for the most part poor illiterates, who no longer felt that they could find in the preaching of their legitimate pastors the message of truth and salvation for which they longed.

The Cathari, moreover, pretended to stand for the authentic tradition of the Apostles. They called themselves Christians and held that they were in fact the true Christians, the *pure ones,* for this is the meaning of the word *katharoi* in Greek. And the *perfect,* by exemplifying, or even improving on, this or that evangelical counsel, appeared to the unobservant to be the most faithful disciples of the Gospel.

As a substitute for the seven sacraments, moreover, they had the quasi-magical rite of the *consolamentum.* One of the *perfect* had but to lay his hands on any *believer,* at the moment of death, and that person would find his soul automatically purified of all sin and freed from all punishment, whether in this world or in the next. A certain number of believers, admittedly, were attracted by the desire to be perfect and devoted themselves sincerely and ardently to the prolonged and difficult mortifications necessary for the reception of the *consolamentum* before death, but, compared with this elite, how many others there were who were taken in by the deceptive lure of a spurious hope! In the fond belief that they could enjoy the blessing of a final purification, to be offered to them unconditionally at the time of death, the latter regarded themselves as dispensed, in this life, from all the normal laws of morality, as well as the commandments of God and those of the Church.

The nobility had swallowed this bait first of all. It was so easy for them to maintain one of the *perfect* in their household, to have ready at hand when their souls had to depart for the next world, to the choirs of angels! But this was by no means the sole advantage which the heresy afforded. Becoming a Cathar meant that one no longer regarded himself under obligation to pay the ecclesiastical tithes. Better still, it was looked upon not only as a permissible, but even as a pious work to pillage the palaces of the bishops or the rich domains of the abbeys.

Little wonder then, under such circumstances, that the counts of Toulouse and Foix, and the viscounts of Beziers and Carcassonne, had become so adept at vacillating between the two currents, endeavoring to avoid the just consequences of excommunication by the Church, while at the same time seeing to it that they would have available the future blessings of a heretical *consolamentum* in their last days. The notorious ambiguity of the Catharist position made it easy for the clever to play this double game. The *perfect*, it appears, were not overly disturbed by such things. And care was taken to keep this important information from the simple mass of the *believers*. This was the depressing state of affairs which the Castilian embassy found prevailing, as they penetrated deeper and deeper into Languedoc. Wherever they went they encountered the dreary spectacle of abandoned churches and pillaged monasteries, and came face to face with thousands who, very often in perfect sincerity, declared that they were the true Christians, the best Christians, and yet who rejected the divinity of Christ and the sign of His cross as a scandal. It is impossible to imagine that either Don Diego or Dominic could have remained indifferent in the midst of such appalling spiritual bankruptcy. "They felt moved by a profound compassion for the many souls who had been led astray by error," one of his earliest biographers notes laconically.

Finally they reached their first stopping place, Toulouse. The episcopal escort, numbering some twenty or thirty knights, could hardly have passed by without arousing local curiosity. In spite of the obvious hostility which they encountered on the faces of he onlookers, it was necessary to find lodgings for the night, either in groups or individually, in the houses of the local inhabitants. One fact is certain, in any case: Dominic's host was a heretic. If there ever has been a truly fateful encounter in the life of man, this was surely one.

How did their discussion open? We do not know. But we do know that it lasted the entire night. Point by point, calmly, with all the assurance of one who knows that he is the intermediary of divine truth, the subprior of Osma refuted the arguments of his opponent. The discussion had nothing of the nature of an oratorical contest. Love alone was the guiding force, the twofold love of God and of a soul in danger of being lost. Dominic was not seeking any personal victory, and his replies were offered without vehemence or bitterness. No attempt at refutation, moreover, by resorting to clever tricks: his appeal was straightforward and clear, the truth of the Gospel cleansed of the gangrenous growth in which the heretics had enveloped it.

"Joyous and elated," Dominic resumed his journey northward. Silence. Prayer. Heart-rending conferences with the Bishop of Osma. Here too the faith was in danger, just as in Spain. But in the latter country, beyond the Sierra Guadarrama, Islam was being driven back by means of the sword. Here, in the Narbonnaise, the persuasive force of truth alone was enough to win over one man. Why not the others?

The words of St. Paul to the Romans[6] took on a new, militant meaning: "For if thou confess with thy mouth that Jesus is the Lord, and believe in thy heart that God has raised him from the dead, thou shalt be saved. . . . How then are they to call upon him in whom they have not believed? But how are they to believe him whom they have not heard? And how are they to hear, if no one preaches?"

"This province has been seduced by so many erroneous doctrines that it must be preached to by a host of preachers," one of the companions of St. Bernard of Clairvaux concluded, a century and a half before, when the saint took him along on an all too brief mission to the Narbonnaise.

"Watchdogs who no longer even know how to bark," exclaimed Pope Innocent III, who had nothing but scorn for the misconduct and indifference of the bishop of Narbonne and his clergy. "Mercenaries who run away and do not pursue the wolf either with their voices or their crooks, soldiers who no longer dare show themselves on the ramparts. . . . They strive to accumulate as many benefices as they can themselves, and confer the priesthood and ecclesiastical offices on unworthy candidates, even on illiterate children!"

Nevertheless, Don Diego went on with the mission with which he had been entrusted. After the consent of the King of Denmark and the young princess in question had been obtained, the Danish court proceeded to seal the bargain by complying with the formalities of a "marriage by proxy." Everything seemed to have gone very well. The Bishop of Osma returned to his diocese and Dominic to his tasks as subprior of the chapter of Osma.

But in the middle of the year 1205 he had to set

out again for the north. Alfonso XIII entrusted to Don Diego the task of escorting the young spouse of the Infante to Spain. With a suite even more numerous and impressive than before, the good bishop again crossed the Pyrenees, made his way through the heretical Narbonnaise, and reached the Marches of Dacia.

However, when the embassy finally reached the Danish court, after many wearisome weeks on the road, they found that the young Danish princess could not be brought back. She had died, according to the chronicles. But if we are to believe the evidence turned up as a result of recent reconsideration of the documents, it appears that she simply refused to go. This should not be at all surprising. Influenced by the tragic example of her aunt Ingeburga, the wife whom Philip Augustus divorced shortly after their marriage, the princess probably concluded that life in a convent was preferable to exile, a voluntary cloister in her own country was better than the anguishing prospects of a political marriage. Such a hypothesis helps to explain the subsequent actions of the ambassador of the King of Castile. While the latter sent a messenger and a part of his escort back to Alfonso XIII, he himself, accompanied by Dominic, took the road to Rome. The supposition is that he was the bearer of a message to the Pope, which probably had to do with the marriage of the Danish princess, and which the court and bishops of that country felt duty bound to submit to the Holy See.

25

In any case, Don Diego was anxious to present to Innocent III a personal petition of his own. He wished to resign his see and have permission to devote himself henceforth to the conversion of the pagans. For while he and Dominic were making their way through the remote countries of the north, not far from the shores of the Baltic, they made a discovery which greatly impressed them. There were still enormous numbers of virtually uncivilized pagans living in those regions, who were totally ignorant of Christianity. Accustomed to thinking of the Moors as the only infidels, they had not imagined that there were still so many other areas of the world, unknown to them until now, of an ill-defined extent, yet ripe for evangelization. Accustomed as they were to the scene of the *reconquista,* they now beheld with their own eyes preparations being made for an even greater expedition, whose objective was to carry the good news of the Gospel to the very lands of the pagans. They were greatly impressed by the large-scale recruitment taking place, an enrollment of soldiers and apostles for the holy purpose of the conquest of souls, although in different capacities. In the various bishoprics through which they passed on their way north, they could not help being influenced by the great wave of apostolic fervor and missionary zeal which they witnessed. They burned with the desire to be able to join these pioneers who were willing to risk their lives in order to bring the truth of Christ to distant lands. If they could only be permitted to go to the Cumans. If martyrdom were to be their lot, they could hope for nothing better, even if they were to be cut up alive, as had happened not too long before to some of these northern apostles.

Innocent III listened to the Bishop of Osma graciously: he asked them questions about the state of the countries of Christendom through which they had recently passed, twice, in connection with the business of their embassy. Although the Pope was pleased to learn of the missionary efforts under way in the region of the Baltic, he was nevertheless much more concerned about the progress of heresy in the south of France. Innocent III was a Pope who took to heart everything that happened to the Church, its triumphs and its failures.

But to the request of Don Diego he simply said no. And so Dominic and his Bishop resumed their journey to Spain.

Again they were on the road. Through Umbria, Tuscany, and Lombardy. Silence. Prayer. It never occured to either Don Diego or Dominic, of course, to question the wisdom of the Pope's orders. But no one could efface from their hearts the flame of apostolic zeal that was now burning there, and would continue to burn in both of them until the end of their days. The names of those distant peoples to whom the name of the Lord Jesus had not been revealed rang in their ears, as they made their way along the ancient Roman road: Wends, Prussians, Livonians, Esthonians, Cu-

27

mans. "How then are they to call upon him in whom they have not believed? But how are they to believe him whom they have not heard? And how are they to hear, if no one preaches?"

So as they were descending the slopes of the Great Saint Bernard, they felt the zeal for souls burning within them more intensely than ever. Up there, by the shores of the Baltic, there were barbarians to be evangelized; here in France they found heretics to be converted.

Of course they had spoken at great length to Innocent III about the Albigensian heresy. And we can regard it as very probable, historically speaking, that Don Diego was entrusted with a new message on the part of the Supreme Pontiff, which it was easier to transmit orally than by written word. This would explain their stay at the abbey of Cîteaux, and the ceremony in which the Bishop of Osma was symbolically invested with the cowl of the sons of St. Bernard. There was, moreover, the remarkable coincidence, "providential" no doubt, but which the papal directives could also have envisaged, which brought Don Diego and Dominic to Montpellier precisely at the moment when, at the bidding of the Holy See, an important assembly of Cistercians was to be held, "for extirpating unmasked heretics from the Narbonnaise." The fact is historically certain, in any case: the Bishop of Osma was received with obvious deference by the three papal legates who were presiding over the gathering in this town, in June, 1206.

Thus, once again, Don Diego and Dominic found themselves facing the tremendous challenge of the Albigensian heresy, itself the result of an unusually complex set of spiritual, social, political, and religious factors. It seems fairly certain that the heresy would not have become so widespread or virulent if it had not coincided with a period of upheaval through which Europe as a whole was passing at this time. The Latin world had reached one of its most crucial turning points. The rise of new forms of social life had revealed the inadequacies of old institutions. Everywhere the two travelers from Castile could see how new forces were at work threatening to upset the old balance of the feudal order. Towns were being founded, right and left, and at once became the chief economic centers. A new social class came into existence, consisting of the bourgeois, merchants, and craftsmen. The great landed estates saw their economic importance decline as that of the towns increased. The protection supplied by suzerains and the taxes paid by vassals in return had both become intolerable burdens. As a result, the towns sought to free themselves from the control of feudal lords.

Nor were individuals any more willing than the towns to put up with the burdens which they had traditionally borne. Material progress had its counterpart in a new demand for progress in the intellectual

29

sphere. There was now an intense desire for knowledge, discussion, and understanding, kindled and nourished by the frequent commercial exchanges between provinces, and even countries.

The mass of the people, moreover, saw no difference between the the suzerainty of lay lords and that of the clergy, whether bishops or abbots. There was a burning desire to be free of both, on the social level, but this did not imply an equal longing for emancipation or rebellion on the spiritual level. Thirteenth century Europe remained profoundly religious, both by conviction as well as by tradition. The desire for knowledge was for the most part almost unconsciously directed toward the fundamental problems of the faith.

It was the institutions of the Church, in particular, which were not in tune with the rhythm of the new age. The great abbeys continued to be mainly agricultural centers, while the sees consisted of a vast network of temporal interests, the management of which very often consumed all the time of the vicar, to the detriment of his spiritual responsibilities which he, as a shepherd of souls, should have placed before all else. None of the clergy had the training required to cope with the new desire for knowledge on the part of the townsmen. The Christian of those days could not help but be conscious of the glaring contrast between the reality of life and the traditional religion in which he had been brought up.

When the innovators made their appearance,

trained and skilled preachers who were conversant
with the problems of the day, was it not inevitable that
they should find a hearing with such a youthful, enthusiastic, illiterate population? Gradually the heresy
of the Waldenses and Cathari filtered in, like water
through the leaky timbers of a boat. Now the boat was
shipping water on all sides. The Catholic faith was in
grave danger in a Christian kingdom. Witness the cry
of alarm raised by an Archbishop of Narbonne: "The
bark of Peter is about to founder in our diocese!" Or
the following admission of helplessness on the part of
Raymond V, Count of Toulouse, in the year 1177:
"Although I am armed with one of the two divine
swords, I do not know how to restrain or put an end to
all this unbelief, and I am obliged to admit that my
forces are frankly incapable of coping with such a vast
and difficult problem, because the most important
nobles in my territory are infected by this disease and
have influenced a great many people to apostasize from
the faith, so that I dare not—in fact, I cannot—do anything about the situation."

Less than twenty-five years later, his own son,
Raymond VI, casting aside all restraining influence,
officially espoused the cause of the heresy and became
one of its most ardent defenders and apostles.

The situation seemed both tragic and hopeless,
especially when we realize that in the feudal Christendom of those days the spiritual and the temporal
powers were so closely allied that it was practically

impossible to separate them. The papacy could then no more be thought of as without temporal power, than the power committed to princes or seigneurs could be thought of as purely political in nature. If every suzerain lord, however low on the social scale, held his rights and powers from the Pope himself, to the extent that they represented a portion of the divine authority committed to the latter, his suzerainty made him, by the same token, the appointed defender of the Catholic faith in his own fief. He was responsible for it before men and before God.

Consequently, he was entrusted with both the right and the duty of placing the armed forces under his command at the disposal of the Church, should the necessity arise. A double-edged sword, whose handling required an unusual amount of prudence! Moreover, it was not permissible to keep it safely sheathed, no matter how much one might wish to do so. It was part of the duty expected of every feudal lord to compel his subjects to respect their baptismal promises, to expel heretics from his lands, if this seemed necessary, or even to put them to death. If he tried to evade these responsibilities he himself would become liable to the sanctions of the Church, of which one of the first would be excommunication. And if penalties of a spiritual nature were insufficient to compel him to act, the Church had power to proceed against him in the purely temporal sphere by releasing his subjects from their oath of fealty to him and by depriving him of his title, his authority, and his lands. As a last resort, in case of obstinate rebellion, the Apostolic See could authorize the preaching of an armed crusade against him. The twenty-seventh canon of the Third Lateran Council had expressly sanctioned this.

Measures of this kind are repugnant to our modern way of thinking, but they were justifiable in the light of a society that was officially Christian and which claimed to be based on a public profession of the Christian faith. Moreover, the dangers threatening this faith were considered, not without reason, as the most fearful of all, because they jeopardized the eternal salvation of souls and must therefore be the first to be eliminated. Yet lofty as the premises were, their application, in concrete circumstances, was fraught with terrible risks, for human passions can so poison the atmosphere that the remedy becomes at times worse than the evil disease itself.

As a matter of fact, while the Church carefully stood by its rights in this field, it favored the use of brute force only when other methods had manifestly failed. In 1198, therefore, in the hope that these wandering sheep could be brought back to the fold by persuasion rather than by force, Pope Innocent III entrusted the Cistercians with the task of preaching to the heretics in the Narbonnaise.

Unfortunately, the heresy had such deep roots in the country after forty years that it could no longer be extirpated by mere sermons, discussions, or *colloquies!*

Heretical councils were being held in broad daylight. Houses of women had been founded, on the order of religious communities, for the daughters of the nobility. The latter kept alive the flame of heretical doctrine and zealously prepared for the final triumph of Catharism by undertaking the education of the children and adolescents. To them the nobles willingly entrusted the training of their own children. Among these women, moreover, there were some whose zeal and sincerity had led them to embrace the heresy and who had willingly put up with the harsh discipline it imposed. Convinced *perfects* themselves, they were remarkably adept at convincing others. Some of their names—such as those of: Faïs Durfort, Blanche de Laurac, Esclarmonde—became famous and in some cases evoke tragic memories.

Because they had expelled Faïs from the city of Pamiers, where the Count of Foix, her brother, had established her with a Catharist community under his care, the canons of Saint-Antoine were made to suffer a terrible fate. One of them was cut to pieces at the foot of the altar as he was celebrating the sacrifice of the Mass. Another had had his eyes gouged out. All the others were driven from their pillaged monastery and compelled to flee, half naked, through the fields and the woods.

It is not difficult to appreciate, therefore, that the task of those who had resolved to combat the heresy by opposing it merely with spiritual means, in accordance with the wishes of Innocent III, was made extremely difficult by the rebellious state of the nobility, the lawlessness of the masses, the intellectual ferment, and the fanatical obstinacy which are responsible for most religious quarrels. When Fulk reached his see of Toulouse, in the same year (1205), he found it a "dead diocese." His life was even in danger. Thirty years before, at Béziers, the heretic townsmen had assassinated their own lord in the church of St. Mary Magdalen, because he had been guilty, in their eyes, of siding with the Catholics. The bishop who had gone to the assistance of the viscount had had his jaw smashed. In short, the attempt to combat or even to track down the heresy without calling on the secular arm to support the apostolic effort was tantamount to becoming involved in a hopeless struggle, humanly speaking, and to court the risk of martyrdom.

3

The Apostolic Preaching

These were the serious questions being considered by the three papal legates, Arnaud Amaury, Abbot General of the Cistercian Order, Pierre de Castelnau and Master Raoul, two monks of the abbey of Fontroide, when Don Diego and Dominic arrived at Montpellier. Depressed by the enormous task beyond their powers and discouraged by repeated failures, the legates would gladly have tendered their resignations to Rome. If any headway were to be made, the Abbot of Cîteaux felt that it could be achieved only through the use of strong measures including the threat of the stake. Pierre de Castelnau, a trained canonist, still hoped that a rigorous application of the canons of the Church would be capable of restoring peace to the province and truth to minds.

However, the Bishop of Osma did not agree with these proposals, and his companion no doubt shared his views. Innocent III had not intended that the mission which he had entrusted to the Cistercians was to be carried out in such a brutal way. Fully aware of the complexity of the problem and without ruling out a priori any of the ways in which the Church could punish sinners according to canon law, he remained and wished to remain, above all, a pastor of souls, especially of souls who have strayed from the truth, for they were the ones most likely to be lost. Don Diego could not help recalling the way in which the Pope had insisted on the phrase the "ministry of the word" and "doctrinal teaching." Men who had been seduced by error were to be convinced by the preaching of the Gospel. The evil could be thoroughly eradicated only by the stronger attraction of the truth in all its glory.

Master Raoul was not opposed in principle to this plan for purely spiritual action. He, much more than the other two legates, felt a deeper sympathy with the ideas of Don Diego and Dominic.

Bit by bit, however, the three Cistercians gradually came to an agreement, which they all more or less shared, upon the primary importance of preaching. One question remained, however, which they were

unable to ignore, namely, how could they overcome the
basic objection of the Cathari to any kind of Catholic
preacher at all, in view of the ignorance, unworthiness,
and indifference of the Catholic clergy? Would it not
be more prudent, as a consequence, to begin the mission by directing their efforts, first, toward the reform
of bishops and priests, whose mere presence, in the
eyes of the heretics, was enough to make the apostolate
of authentic preachers completely futile? No, replied
the bishop of Osma, firmly. The work of preaching
must by all means go on, directed at every level of
society, for it constituted in the words of Pope Innocent III an "absolute necessity." Besides, it was completely illusory to imagine that it was possible to
restore the clergy and episcopate of the Narbonnaise
completely to a state of perfection acccording to norms
dictated by the Cathari. Even supposing that it were
possible to find Catholic ministers who were perfect
according to the standards normally expected of them,
by what right could one ask them to devote themselves
to the heroic practice of the evangelical counsels,
particularly of poverty, which the Church does not
impose on them?

One solution and one solution alone could meet
the difficulties raised by this particular problem,
namely, that preachers commissioned by the Church
should consent to assume, on their own responsibility,
the burden of strict conformity to the evangelical
counsels: they must take a vow to conform to the

apostolic life as perfectly as they could, and should set out on their journeys, two by two, as true poor in Christ, without money, even going so far as to beg for their daily bread. What objection could the heretics then have when faced by exemplary missionaries of this kind?[7]

Very much amazed, the three papal legates listened to this unheard-of proposal in silence. For monks, abbots, legates of the Pope publicly to adopt such a manner of life was regarded in the thirteenth century as a preposterous and even revolutionary suggestion. If a religious were to presume to work as a common stevedore on the wharves of Marseilles today, in the twentieth century, we would be no less shocked. No, regardless of how well founded the solution proposed by such a person as the Bishop of Osma was, the Cistercians "could not by themselves adopt such a method, which smacked too much of novelty."

Feudal society maintained that the very dignity of the Church demanded that its prelates should live with an external splendor equal to that of the secular princes, the wielders of temporal power, in the belief that unless they did so Christendom might forget the spiritual basis of the Church's power and authority.

It was not, as has so often been implied, a fear of austerity or poverty on the part of individuals that caused the legates of Montpellier to raise their eyebrows at the new suggestion. The austerities practiced in the six hundred monasteries of the Order were

39

just as rigorous as those of which the Cathari *perfect* made so much. Rather, they were frightened by the novelty of appearing in public in a way which would have made them seem like those unauthorized preachers who, for a century now, had been wandering over the roads of medieval Europe like the wandering monks of old (*gyrovagi*).

Neither Amaury nor Pierre de Castelnau, much less Master Raoul, had any intention, of course, of decrying the value of truly evangelical poverty for those who wished to preach in the province of Narbonne. Men of goodwill do not find it difficult to admit the logic of the perfectly obvious. Therefore, once they had gotten over their initial amazement, the Cistercians no longer dared assert that "by its novelty, the thing is impossible." If some person of real moral authority agreed to go before them, preaching in the manner suggested, they concluded, they would willingly follow him.

With his characteristic and spontaneous zeal, the Bishop from Castile then arose. If someone must begin in this way—and there was no doubt on this point— he was ready himself to assume the risk. His decision made, he at once sent back to his diocese the rest of the escort which he had kept after leaving Denmark, including his luggage, horses, and servants. Only the subprior of his chapter, who was more enthusiastic than anyone for the idea of apostolic preaching, would remain with him.

No indication has come down to us regarding Dominic's precise reaction or his words on this occasion. But Etienne de Bourbon much later furnished an important observation with regard to these events: "This was the first seed of the Order of the Preachers. I have heard this asserted by the first brothers who were in that land with blessed Dominic."

The resolute attitude of the Bishop of Osma finally convinced the Cistercian legates. But because Amaury was obliged to return to Cîteaux in order to attend a coming Chapter General of his Order, Don Diego at once found himself obliged to take over the direction of the missionaries as well as the mission. As for Dominic, laying aside both his charge and title of subprior of the chapter of Osma, he became simply "brother Dominic."

A messenger was dispatched to Rome to inform the Pope, without delay, of the grave decisions which had been reached in the assembly of Montpellier, and to obtain his approval of what had been decided. Pierre de Castelnau and Master Raoul sent their followers, horses, and luggage back to Fontfroide. They kept only the books necessary for chanting the canonical office and those which would be needed in helping them prepare for the forthcoming disputes or *colloquies* with the heretics. They intended, at once, to take up the challenge of the Cathari, to beat them at their own game, and to employ their own tactics in order to convince them.

Relieved of all belongings, like true beggars, the four missionaries set out boldly for the very heart of heretical country. They entered the viscounty of Béziers, where one of the most fearful of their opponents resided, Etienne de Servian, who boasted of harboring on his lands the most illustrious preachers of the sect. Toward the beginning of July, Don Diego was able to obtain permission for a public colloquy in the town of Servian.

The people of those days took a passionate interest in these oratorical jousts in which the different sides struggled against each other by means of Scriptural texts, with attack and reply rolling out like artillery charges. If the disputes could not be held in one of the great halls of the castle, they took place on a special platform erected for the purpose in the open air. The lord of the place usually presided. Referees were chosen in advance, who were to decide at the end of the colloquy as to the truth of the arguments alleged by one or the other side. Sometimes the sessions were prolonged for eight consecutive days, and on occasion even for fifteen. And they were not without considerable risk for the antagonists. The reaction of the mob was unpredictable, as it trembled, hanging on every word, always prepared to turn with gruesome violence against champions who did not measure up to their expectations. In some cases the hearers had even been known to ignite a pyre with their own hands and cast the vanquished contestants into the flames.

The Cathari, moreover, were not above resorting

to crafty and wily methods of debating, and the local lord always knew how to make his influence felt. Even if the heretics were proved wrong, they could still count on his support, if he were pleased to defend them. As a result of his threats, whether overt or veiled, the generous zeal for the good of souls, loyal but weak, was in danger of very soon falling, like the flames of the pyre, illumined for an instant by the delirious enthusiasm of a fickle crowd.

This is the way things went at Servian. After eight days of bitter debate, it was the attitude of the lord, Etienne, which deprived Don Diego and his companions of the victory that was their right.

The missionaries, nevertheless, did not hesitate to continue their dangerous journey. They reached Béziers, where fifteen days of disputation ended in a draw. Pierre de Castelnau appeared to be too rigid and threats of death were heard being uttered against his person. It was thought more prudent for him to withdraw, for a time at least. After Béziers, they went on to Carcassonne, guarded by its walls with their crenelated towers and machicolations. This place was a veritable citadel of the Catharist heresy, whose citizens, it was said, were "the worst heretics and sinners in the sight of God." Next they proceeded to Toulouse by way of Lavaur and Verfeuil. "Verte-Feuille, may God wither you!" This was the curse uttered by the lips of St. Bernard of Clairvaux, a century before, when he encountered the hardheartedness of the small town.

In the spring of 1207, Diego, Raoul, and Dominic

made their way to the citadel of Montréal for a major dispute. Pierre de Castelnau joined them there. The battle here would be very difficult; the result could have a considerable bearing on the course of their mission. The lord of the place, Aimery of Montréal, would preside over the colloquy. The Cathari had summoned their most famous champions. There were four persons on each side ready for the contest, surrounded, as was customary, by a impressive number of collaborators. There were also four judges, who had been chosen with the approval of Aimery from among the *believers* or promoters of the heresy alone. At the start, therefore, the advantage was, humanly speaking, on the side of the heterodox. Conscious of their strength, one of the Catharistic deacons rudely opened the debate with the assertion that the Roman Church was the Babylon, mother of fornications and abominations, which St. John the Evangelist had seen in his great vision of the Apocalypse. Don Diego took up the challenge and went on to counterattack. Brother Dominic was left to assume part of the burden of defense.

For fifteen days the struggle was waged back and forth, tenaciously, zealously, followed day after day by an impassioned audience. This was one of the most famous of these theological jousts and the only one about which we have any detailed knowledge. The Scriptural arguments on which both sides relied were submitted in writing. The replies of opponents were in turn written out and then followed by new rebuttals. Both before and after each session, the *libellus* had to be carefully drawn up and then handed to the judges to study, at their leisure and to pronounce their authoritative decision.

It was apparently at the colloquy of Montréal that a certain well known incident took place, described in the written account of Pierre des Vaux Cernai.

Between two sessions, the heretics were sitting by the fire and preparing the presentation of their case. "One of them to whom Dominic had given the paper containing his arguments handed it in turn to his companions. The latter suggested that the piece of paper be thrown into the fire. If the fire burned it, that could be taken as a sign that their case was the true one. If, on the contrary, it did not burn, the Cathari were prepared to admit the justice of the Catholic case. Soon all had agreed on this procedure. The piece of paper was accordingly thrown into the fire. But although it remained among the flames for some time, it emerged without having been burned even in the slightest degree. Naturally all were greatly amazed" by this result, but they were not convinced. The paper was thrown in a second time, and then a third time. But each time the paper "emerged whole and unscathed."

The Church—it must be stressed in passing—has never approved acts of this kind, even though bishops or local councils have sometimes resorted to them here and there. Those who have felt there was justification for having recourse to the *ordeal* or "judgment of God" have always done so, whether they were aware of it or not, in opposition to papal directives on the subject. The Cathari, of course, had no scruples of this kind. But—and this point is worth noting—by choosing a *simpliste* and childish device they thought to dispense themselves from the necessity of studying a document which would have refuted their doctrinal positions.

No such deception, however, was employed by the witness who received this account—he tells us so himself—"from a knight who belonged to the above-mentioned Cathari and already was somewhat inclined to our faith; this is why he was not willing to hide what he had just seen and disclosed it to several persons." The heretics "swore one another to secrecy about a miracle" which was so disastrous for their cause. To avoid sanctioning the defeat of their own side, the judges considered it more prudent to suspend the debate without offering a verdict. But the *libellus* of Brother Dominic was carefully preserved by his adversaries, because they were afraid to allow the circulation of a document which, by its nature, amounted to a double defeat for them.

The hasty retreat of the advocates of the sect, in addition to the masterly defense of the papal missionaries, brought back to the fold of the Church some one hundred and fifty wandering sheep. A foothold had been gained, in spite of all, which must be exploited, without delay, in order to reach the châteaux and surrounding villages by preaching.

Now in the spring of this same year of 1207, the preachers received an unexpected reinforcement. In response to the appeal addressed to their whole Order three years before, twelve Cistercian abbots disembarked on the banks of the Rhone, in the neighborhood of Beaucaire. "Without money for the journey, without horses, armed only with the prestige of knowledge and eloquence," desirous above all to reveal themselves as "men of the Gospel," they came to found the *Holy Preaching of Jesus Christ.*

Arnaud Amaury, therefore, now found himself at the head of an élite troop, supported by the companions which each of the abbots had brought with him, in all, some forty zealous religious, "ready to defend the faith at all costs." Amaury assigned to each of the abbots a special area in the province and handed them the ecclesiastical mandate authorizing them to take part in public disputes and to preach. A great wave of enthusiasm swept over the teams of missionaries as they dispersed through the Narbonnaise.

Unfortunately, three months had scarcely gone by before the flame was already in danger of being extinguished.

Exhausted by his labors, Master Raoul had been the first to return to the abbey of Franquevaux. By the beginning of July he was dead. One after the other the

47

remaining abbots soon withdrew from the enterprise.
The task, in short, was felt to be beyond their strength.
Moreover, they could devote themselves to it only
provisionally, in much the same way as crusaders who
were often eager to embrace the great adventure only
just long enough to gain the indulgence attached.
Moreover, it was not in accordance with the vocation
of a Cistercian to preach outside his monastery, and
when the results were so meager, what was the use of
persisting in the effort? One of them bitterly exclaimed, "I have to admit—God help me!—these
people care no more for a sermon than for a rotten
apple!"

September, October . . . Then came the great dispersal. But Don Diego did not give up. If the "workers
in the vineyard" were wanting in France, he, as Bishop
of Osma, would return to Castile to gather new recruits. Moreover, it was particularly urgent for him to
go there now to attend to the affairs of his diocese after
an absence of more than two years. After engaging
once more in the fray of a colloquy at Pamiers, the one
that forms the basis, to all intents and purposes, for
the *Holy Preaching of Narbonnaise,* he crossed the
Pyrenees.

Between Montréal and Fanjeaux, in the little hamlet of Prouille, the very heart of enemy territory, there
was no one left but Brother Dominic with Guillaume
Claret, a young priest, as his sole companion.

Then, suddenly, in the same fortnight of January,

1208, two dreadful pieces of news reached Prouille: Don Diego had died at Osma on December 30th of the preceding year, and on January 14th, Pierre de Castelnau had been felled by the murderous dagger of one of the heretics. Only Dominic now remained in the field to confront the heretics. He was only thirty-six years old at the time.

"He was a person of medium height, with a slightly ruddy complexion, blond yellow hair, almost red. His forehead seemed to give off a glow which gained him the reverence and affection of others. He always appeared to be gentle and happy, unless moved by compassion for the suffering of some neighbor. He had long, beautifully shaped hands, and a strong, pleasant, well modulated voice." This is the description of him left us by Sister Caecilia, one of his spiritual daughters in Rome, who came to know him in 1220. But he must already have appeared this way toward the end of January, 1208, when the task for which God had reserved him, without his full awareness, was just beginning.

In terra deserta, et invia et inaquosa . . .

This hostile province in an alien country would become for him the desert without way and without water, even more than the Castilian plain of his childhood. A land spiritually parched, for the waters of life brought by Christ no longer flowed there: This is everlasting life, that they may know thee, . . . and him whom thou hast sent, Jesus Christ."[9] A trackless land where the thorns of error had already blotted out even the traces of the path of truth . . . A desert land, because God was no longer known there, no longer loved . . . "O Lord, what is to become of sinners?"

It would be folly, even presumption, to think that one man could cope with such an enormous task alone under the circumstances. Unless, of course, one were looking at things not from the viewpoint of man but of God. "True mystics," said Bergson, "simply open themselves to the wave which floods them. Sure of themselves, because they feel in themselves something greater than themselves, they reveal themselves as great men of action, to the surprise of those for whom mysticism is nothing more than a vision, a transport, an ecstasy." This is because "the love which consumes them is no longer simply the love of a man for God, it is the love of God for all men."[10]

4

Prouille: In the Eye of the Hurricane

Until now Brother Dominic had played a purely secondary role in the apostolic activity of the mission to the Narbonnaise, just as he had not had any part himself in the choice which made him a companion of the Bishop of Osma on the great mission which took him from the cloister of Osma and caused him to travel twice over the roads of Europe. He had always remained an "assistant" of his Bishop, merely a canon regular, moreover, among a group composed exclusively of monks.

However, Providence had willed that his post

should bring him to the hamlet of Prouille as the companion of Don Diego, a small place which had become a kind of base camp for the mission ever since 1207. The itinerant preachers had needed a rallying point, a place where they could come, periodically, to recoup their strength, both on a spiritual and a physical level. The Cathari also possessed "hospices" of this kind, such as the one at Fanjeaux, which were often run by communities of women *perfects,* and which were well endowed with temporal revenues, for the purpose of assuring the existence and development of the sect. Prouille fulfilled a similar function for the Catholic missionaries, and as a matter of fact the name of *Holy Preaching* very soon became attached to it, although the term still continued to be used for the mission and its members as a whole.

It was at Prouille that the converted heretics received their letters of reconciliation. One of the tasks of Brother Dominic was precisely to make these out, then to affix the round seal of white wax used by ecclesiastical tribunals.

It was at Prouille also that in the first year of the apostolate a community of women was founded, due to the initiative of Don Diego, who had been compelled by the force of circumstances to follow the tactics of the Cathari in this respect. Once the women and young daughters of the nobility had been converted, how could one prevent them from relapsing into their old ways or assure their material welfare, except by providing them with some kind of residence?

For most of them, breaking with the heresy actually amounted to breaking with their families. It was therefore not at all surprising that this asylum should gradually be transformed into a monastery, if we bear in mind the attraction which the spiritual life exercised on such a large number of Christians in those days. Without this attraction, the proselytism of the Cathari would not have had the success that it did in the Narbonnaise. But, on the other hand, their proselytism, in spite of the doctrinal errors propagated by the sect, aroused in pure souls a thirst for God and the desire for an authentic perfection.

Therefore Fulk, bishop of Toulouse, had granted to the *Holy Preaching* the chapel and enclosure of Notre-Dame de Prouille, a providential first step toward a work, whose greatness no one as yet suspected. It seemed rather that the hurricane which was gathering on the horizon was about to carry off the small remainder of the mission, like a piece of straw in the wind.

The assassination of Pierre de Castelnau, the Papal Legate, shocked Christian France. It was no longer possible to temporize with the enemies of the Church. Raymond, Count of Toulouse, was held responsible for the murder. Innocent III was no longer content to thunder out a new decree of excommunication against him: he relieved his vassals of their oath of fidelity and "exposed his land for the taking." He then launched a solemn appeal for a crusade. Philip Augustus was invited to assume the direction of the holy war, but as King of France he was caught between the threatening pincers of England and the Holy Roman Empire and refused the leadership, but he gave his barons permission to take the cross.

And so, to the sound of the clanking of arms, the preliminaries of a bloody campaign were made. The preparations lasted one full year—a year of nightmare for the people of the Narbonnaise, a year of espionage, pursuit, and hatred.

By June, 1209, the crusaders had reached Lyons. Pilgrims? Warriors? Both in succession, or both together. An army that soon turned into a fanatical horde, which no longer knew whether it was armed for the cause of God or merely for its own personal gain, whether it wielded the sword to defend right, or simply to indulge in murder—to strike, kill, destroy. At Béziers, there was an orgy of massacre and frenzied pillaging. Thousands of innocent persons fell victim; crowds of women and children fled in terror. Raymond Roger held out for two weeks behind the stout walls of Carcassonne, but, at the end of his resources, he too was obliged to beg for mercy. The inhabitants of the town who were able to escape lost all their possessions. Raymond VI of Toulouse, who, to all intents and purposes, had unleashed the storm, withdrew like an unworthy coward and by means of solemn promises—

which he could not and would not keep—escaped from
the clutches of the crusade against him, and even went
so far as to take the cross himself, the height of
cowardice and perfidy.

However, his nephew, Raymond Roger, was declared *faidit*,[11] dispossessed. Simon de Montfort, the
earl of Leicester, a man of unquestioned valor, received
without qualms the lands and rights of the dispossessed
nephew and took over the supreme command of the
crusade. Two years later, in 1211, he was also invested
with the heritage of the count of Toulouse, who had
failed to keep his promises and found himself like his
nephew, excommunicated and *faidit*, deprived of his
fief. But Peter II of Aragon, the suzerain of the greater
part of these southern territories, who had until now
fought in the army of the crusaders, was afraid of the
inordinate ambition of Simon de Montfort and went
over to the other side to defend his vassals.

On the 12th of September, 1213, the famous battle
of Muret, in which Peter II was killed, took place.
The war nevertheless went on. The hostilities spread
farther and farther; passions became more and more
embroiled. In exasperation the ardor of religious exalta-
tion turned into fanaticism. Among the crusaders as
well as the heretic *perfects*, there were undoubtedly
some who, in complete sincerity, offered themselves
to God, "body and soul," before going into battle.
Montfort was one of these. Monks, bishops, papal
legates hastened with the crowds into the churches

and while the battle was raging, prayed, sang hymns, and sought God's help. The supplication of prayer was raised on high to the sound of the fray. Both sides were convinced that they were defending the right: all excesses seemed justified.

Between the Pope and his legates there developed a difference of opinion. Innocent III had never expected that the struggle would assume its present scope, would be carried on with such violence, or would last so long. The Pope had not proclaimed the holy war so that one man, even the loyal Simon de Montfort, could conquer, for his own personal advantage, a territory the size of a kingdom. The holy war had become an accursed war. He had hoped that it would bring order and peace; instead it had raised up man against man, and, for purely earthly reasons, the subjects of the king of Aragon against the French barons. The people of Toulouse refused to recognize the Earl of Montfort as their suzerain. Five years after the battle of Muret, the siege of Toulouse took place. On June 25, 1208, Simon de Montfort was struck on the head by a stone which pierced his temple. "When he died, everything collapsed," an old chronicle laconically observed. However, the hurricane had spared the *Holy Preaching* of Prouille. Paradoxical as this may seem, it is a fact. It is sometimes implied that Brother Dominic took part, on a limited scale, in the crusade against the *Albigenses*. Some have even maintained that he was by the side of Montfort at Muret, obtaining by his prayers the defeat of the opposing army. But nothing of the kind happened.

The truth is that a man such as he was could not fail to bear the mark of his age. Because he was a man of his time, it was impossible for him to condemn the crusade, in principle at least. Appealing to arms in order to defend the cause of God was considered legitimate in those days. For four centuries now, in his own country, an armed struggle had been carried on to reconquer the territories occupied by the infidels. But just as the thought never occurred to him to join the *reconquistadores* in Spain, so it did not occur to him to take his place beside the crusaders in France, even though he became the friend of Simon de Mont-fort.

He was convinced that his vocation was not the same as theirs. His sole task was to bring to men the spiritual message of the Gospel, with means which were uniquely spiritual, in the name of the mandate given him by the Church. Neither the upheaval which came in the wake of the Albigensian crusade, nor the risks which he encountered on this account, could deter him from his purpose. Without regard for danger, fatigue, rebuffs, and reverses he went peacefully on with his journeys to Servian, Béziers, Carcassonne, Montréal, Fanjeaux, Lavaur, Toulouse, Castres, Pamiers. For nearly ten years, day after day, he could be seen wending his way along the roads and lanes, always wearing the same tunic of white wool and the same black cape with its hood, worn, mended, heavy under the summer sun, or soaked from the fall or winter rains. He had neither purse nor bag but went with only a staff in his hand and in the folds of his tunic the Gospel of St. Mathew and the Epistles of St. Paul. Truly poor in Christ, he set out for the conquest of souls, hoping to win all to Jesus Christ, "for in his heart there was an amazing, almost unbelievable desire for the salvation of all men." For this reason, nothing seemed too hard for him.

Unquestionably he understood from the very first that to refute the errors of the heretical preachers effectively, it was necessary to conform oneself to their austerity. But even more than this consideration, it was his vehement desire to resemble Christ the Redeemer which governed his daily mortifications: love which goes further and is stronger even than death, which often threatened, but a love so sweet that his face sometimes seemed to glow.

The facts naïvely recorded by those who chanced to behold him at this time have an incomparable freshness. A woman who gave lodging to the missionary in the course of his wanderings was astounded to find the bed always as she had made it up the evening before, because Brother Dominic spent his nights in prayer. And if, perchance, it was necessary to grant some thought to sleep, he simply rolled up in his cape and lay down on the bare ground.

His frugality, moreover, did not escape the attentive eye of his hostess: "I never knew him to eat during the same meal more than a quarter of a fish or more than two yolks of an egg; nor drink more than a glass of wine mixed with three parts of water; nor eat more than one slice of bread." Once a ferryman became angry because he did not have the wherewithal to pay for his passage over the river and saw him suddenly stoop down and pick up a penny which happened to be there, one knew not how. There was the fisherman who caught on the end of his hook, intact and perfectly dry, the two books which Dominic had lost in the water as he was wading across a stream, despite the deep water and very strong current.

One day he left for a colloquy, accompanied by the local Bishop. Both had removed their shoes as an act of penitence and poverty. An unknown guide offered to direct them, but out of malice led them by way of a road covered with thorns and brambles. Joyously Brother Dominic went on, exulting: "We can hope for victory, for already our sins are washed in blood!" This saying, of course, is not so expressive of valor as a sword blow received but, repeated a hundred, a thousand times or more, over months and years, what force do acts of this kind not have! Their guide that day did not wait for the dispute to rally with conviction to the side of the Gospel.

Brother Dominic would willingly and joyously have given all his blood to bring back wandering souls to the truth! He knew full well that there were some among the heretics who had vowed his death. One evening, between Prouille and Fanjeaux, he ran into a trap. Two men lay in ambush in the underbrush. Dominic was not unaware of what was happening and sang as loud and as joyously as he could while making his way along the winding road. What could he desire more than martyrdom? The words of the hymn—the "Veni Creator" or the "Ave Maris Stella"—resounded in the solitude and amazed the assassins who were ready to strike. It was impossible to attack a man who advanced toward death with such "joyous calm." They let him pass. But his enemies a little later could not resist questioning him about the incident and asked the preacher directly: "If we had struck you down, what would you have done?"—"I would have asked you not to kill me at one blow, but to prolong my martyrdom by mutilating my members one by one. Then to have caused my eyes to behold, one by one, the severed members. Then to tear out my eyes. Finally, to let my torso bathe in its own blood or to finish me off altogether."

Dominic was not boasting when he said this. It was certainly not a question of "the typical Spanish boastfulness of a fanatic," as one modern author suggests. It was a well known fact that one of the canons of Saint-Antoine de Pamiers had suffered this kind of torture, and Dominic was certainly aware of it. He knew also the lengths to which the sadism of certain lords could go, who took delight in the daily torture of unarmed crusaders who were captured on their lands. Above all he knew that the love of the Lord Jesus did not recoil from the inhuman torture of the crucifixion. Everything that could make him like Christ, the Redeemer of all men, Dominic yearned to experience himself. That is why "he received injuries like a choice gift and great recompense." He explained why he was more willing to linger in the region of Carcassonne than in that of Toulouse as follows: "At Toulouse I find many people who honor me, while at Carcassonne everybody opposes me." No matter how much people cried out against him, spat in his face, threw mud and ordure on him, he went serenely on with his travels and his preaching. Hunger, thirst, heat, cold, the icy waters of the rivers which he was sometimes obliged to cross by swimming, the howling of hungry wolves in the woods through which he passed, nothing, in short, could disturb his peace of mind. What was there for him to fear, since his only ambition was to suffer like Christ and with Him for the salvation of the world? His attitude was characterized neither by fanaticism nor stoicism, but by a zeal for souls which was apparent in his gestures, his words, and his looks, and which ultimately touched souls and brought them back to God. One account tells us that "when he preached, he did so with such tremendous effect, that very often he himself was moved to tears and caused his listeners to weep." "Never," our witness also notes, "have I heard anyone

61

whose words were capable of arousing repentance so effectively." Toward those he thirsted to reconcile with God he always maintained an astonishing mercy and a love overflowing with tenderness.

Brother Dominic did this in spite of the tremendous activity which henceforth was to occupy him for almost the rest of his life, because he always retained, in his inner soul, an unbroken communion with God. He recited the canonical hours as he went along the road, or pursued his prayer in silence. If he came to a church or monastery, he entered and took part with the monks in chanting the office. When the day did not leave him enough time for long hours of prayer, he made up for this at night. Before speaking of God to men, he spoke first of men to God, for God alone can change hearts. At Saint-Antoine de Pamiers, as formerly at Osma, he was heard to utter deep groans while at prayer. At Saint-Paul de Narbonne there was the same supplication which rose in great cries, piercing the silence of the night: "Lord, have pity on your people! What is to become of sinners?"

The more pressing the demands of his apostolate, the more urgent the need for prayer. The one could only be the overflowing of the other, for otherwise there was the risk of not getting beyond the level of purely human activity. How could one quench the thirst of those who were dying of thirst, if one did not remain oneself in contact with the source.

For this reason also Brother Dominic resolved to

associate the nuns of Prouille with his work of preaching. They would certainly not be preachers of the Word in fact, but they could be preachers by means of a life of prayer and penance in the cloister, in union with the *Holy Preaching*. A more efficacious help, in fact, than the sword of the crusaders. Dominic had an intuition of this from the very first. Despite his incessant travels, he succeeded in establishing both the material and spiritual foundations of a monastery, while gathering about him a number of new companions. There were five in 1214. He accepted new donations, indispensable for carrying on the work. Fulk, Bishop of Toulouse, was the first to approve his plans. Then, in the course of the years 1215 and 1218, he obtained the confirmation of the Holy See, both for the community of women and for the missionary center of the *Preaching of Saint-Romain de Toulouse*.

Although he was in charge of both groups, he was commonly called the Prior of Prouille. That is what he actually was. To those who urged him to accept this or that bishopric made vacant by the activities of the crusade, his reply was that he "could not neglect the young plantation of Prouille," and he declined, one after the other, the offers which they made to him.

Although he was not able to win striking victories over all the heretics, the *Holy Preaching*, thanks to him, took deeper and more solid root in the Church of God.

God, moreover, was pleased, from time to time, to

depart from the laws of nature on his behalf. A sick canon suddenly recovered his health when Brother Dominic laid his hands on him. Or again a blind man was cured of his affliction. A certain Berengaria assures us that she saw with her own eyes the devil take flight, under the form of a monstrous cat, while the prior of Prouille was catechizing the new converts. A possessed man was delivered of an evil spirit by his prayers. Twice Dominic himself, with one of his companions, mysteriously entered a house whose doors were firmly locked.

But the most marvelous miracle, without doubt, was that of the preacher who "consecrated himself with his whole strength and with burning zeal to win for Christ as many souls as possible," who "bears in the inner sanctuary of his compassion the misfortunes of his brethren," and "always remains ready to announce the Word of God, by day or by night, in churches or houses, in the fields or on the roads, trying to walk in the footsteps of the "Lord Jesus, Saviour of all men, who devoted Himself entirely to our salvation."

At the end of the terrible drama of the Albigensian Crusade, a council met at Montpellier in January, 1215, under the presidency of Peter of Benevento, papal legate *a latere,* sent by Innocent III to bring peace to the Narbonnaise. Pastoral as well as political questions were discussed. Dominic took part in the assembly along with Fulk. Still attached juridically to the chapter at Osma, he attended in his capacity as Prior of Prouille, the head of a monastery of nuns, and was accompanied, moreover, by two or three of his brethren.

5

The Order of Preachers: The Beginnings

But the hour had finally come when, under the irresistible impulse of an inner call and in response to the course of events, the Prior of Prouille was about to be transformed into the founder of a religious Order. At a pace unique till then in the annals of the Church, a handful of men united in the sole aim of opposing error by preaching the truth of the Gospel was about to multiply and spread across the world, with amazing rapidity and effectiveness.

Dominic visited Toulouse in 1215. There, thanks to his efforts, a new monastery of women had been established, whose members no longer consisted of former Catharistic *perfects*, but of repentant girls saved from prostitution. Moreover, a townsman named Pierre Seila donated to Dominic certain buildings which belonged to him and then gave himself to God. By a charter dated this same year, Fulk expressly recognized the new foundation and gave it his entire approval. The terms of this document leave no one in doubt regarding the constitution of the new Order being founded, or the purpose which it was intended to serve:

"In the name of our Lord, Jesus Christ, we bring to the knowledge of all, present and to come, that we, Fulk, by the grace of God, humble minister of the see of Toulouse, in order to extirpate the perversion of heresy, to banish vice, to teach the articles of the faith, and to inculcate in men a sound morality, institute in our diocese Brother Dominic and his companions, whose set purpose it is to live as religious by going about on foot and preaching the word of evangelical truth in evangelical poverty."

Shortly after having signed this charter, Fulk left for Rome to attend the Fourth Lateran Council, which Innocent III had summoned for the month of November, 1215. Dominic accompanied him. His intention was to obtain from the Pope the approval of his Order, which was to bear the name of *Ordo Praedicatorum*, and would in fact be just that. The word, "preacher," it is true, was not new. But in the age of St. Gregory the Great it had not signified a religious order, rather a hierarchical class in the Church, namely, that of the bishops, who, by the very fact of their consecration, had received a mandate to teach the doctrines of faith. It was common for various prelates to hand over this mission, for a determined period, to this or that priest in their diocese. But to transmit the office of preaching, on a permanent basis, to a religious order composed of clerics was tantamount to taking a step unheard of at the beginning of the thirteenth century. It amounted to a serious innovation, a fundamental change in the pastoral system of the Church, which some held to be nothing less than revolutionary.

Numerous papal directives, however, for at least a quarter of a century had been urging upon the bishops the importance of frequent and sound preaching, telling them expressly to "secure the assistance of virtuous preachers of good sense." The idea was especially dear to Innocent III. The disaster of the Albigensian Crusade, moreover, had proved only too well the virtues of a purely spiritual approach, for the Pope not to lend an attentive ear to the joint request which Fulk and Dominic together had come to present. He therefore approved what had been done orally, without raising any difficulty, and in accordance with the custom of the times ratified the gift made to the priory of Prouille in the land of Narbonnaise. All, however, had not yet been finally settled.

The members of the Council, consisting of no less than three patriarchs, four hundred and twelve bishops, and more than eight hundred abbots and priors, gave special consideration to the related questions of the preaching throughout Christendom and the role of religious orders. One of the canons solemnly promulgated toward the end of November repeated the order to the bishops to find suitable candidates who, under their direction, could carry on the apostolic work of preaching and the priestly ministry in all its forms.

The Pope reminded those who were in charge of the theological training of the clergy of the importance of establishing theological schools connected with chapters or colleges. Dominic was well aware of the danger resulting to other provinces because of the greater splendor of the University of Paris. The latter was so attractive at this time that masters as well as students were virtually fleeing from other centers of learning, which were consequently in danger of collapse.

On the other hand, the Fathers of the Council were disturbed by the increasing number of new religious congregations. The age was witnessing a veritable epidemic of corporations of one kind or another, which were appearing in all classes of society. Besides confraternities of penance or of preachers, corporations of boatmen or of artists, there were also bizarre groups, such as corporations of brigands and highwaymen. Now too much social fermentation was not always a healthy sign. Various religious associations which had sprung up almost everywhere in response to trends

69

more or less controlled by the hierarchy, had turned into sects or were bordering on schism or heresy. Therefore the Council refused to permit the foundation of any new religious order in the Church. "If anyone desires to enter religion," the thirteenth canon decreed, "let him join one of the orders which have been previously approved. In the same way, if anyone wishes henceforth to found a new religious order, he must adopt the rule and constitution of an approved religious order."

Innocent III, it is true, had the authority to derogate from this decree of the Council in favor of the Prior of Prouille, or he could simply have shown that the Order had been effectively constituted and approved before the opening of the Council. He preferred, however, to abide by the decree that had just been promulgated. It was better, he thought, for Dominic and his companions to choose one of the rules of religious life already in force. In this way he would avoid the danger of arousing grave suspicions which could later hinder the development of his Order. Based on an ancient rule, on the other hand, the Order would have a solid basis. Taking this stand, Innocent III declared that he was disposed to confirm an Order vowed to preaching and approved the name of Preachers which its members had chosen.

In the spring of 1216, Dominic was back in Toulouse and Prouille. His sons and daughters received the comforting news that he brought from Rome with thanksgiving. At Pentecost, it seems, he convoked a kind of foundation chapter. How many were they, these first brethren who were invited to choose freely the rule that was to govern them? Hardly fifteen. A mere seed, yet Dominic had no doubt but that it would grow to be very fruitful.

The brethren unanimously chose the Rule of St. Augustine. This was an extremely flexible rule, already followed by the chapter of Osma, which went right to the heart of the matter by advocating the communal form of life lived by the earliest Christians, as described in the Book of Acts, involving the common ownership of property and the observance of chastity and obedience. A canonical, not a monastic rule, it mentioned the choral recitation of the divine office but was silent about the detailed activities of the community. For twenty years Dominic had allowed himself to be governed by its spirit and had remained faithful to it during the entire time of the Narbonnaise mission.

To the canonical portion of this rule, advocated by the Popes for so many centuries, Dominic proceeded to graft a number of specifically monastic, well chosen customs, borrowed from the constitutions of the Order of the Premonstratensians.

The canonical, regular, and contemplative life, and the ministry of the word, the full plenitude of the apostolic life, in other words, were to find themselves united, rather fused, for the first time, in an original and magnificently articulated synthesis, which was destined to remain the special glory of the Order of Preachers.

"If anyone feels called from the contemplative to an active life," St. Thomas Aquinas was to declare less than fifty years after the foundation of the Order "it is clear that he is not abandoning contemplation, but joining action to it."[12] This is the way Dominic regarded things from the very first. Apostolic action, for him and for his sons, was nothing less than the fullness of an authentic contemplation. That is why, in spite of the urgent need for apostles which he himself had experienced the hard way, he did not hesitate to shore up the ministry of the word by prescribing a life of austerity and prayer, in strict conformity with conventional monastic tradition. For him, the only starting point for preaching was study, silent prayer, humility of heart, and authentic poverty, that is, it must have both a spiritual and a material basis.

It is true that it was a bold idea to wish to reconcile that which seemed irreconcilable—and that which still seems so to many today—but Dominic now knew what the spirit of his Order must be. He knew what he wanted by having learned it through experience. He knew by the profound supernatural instinct of a soul totally sensitive to the inspiration of the Holy Spirit. He knew that neither the austerity of the regular life nor the obligations of the liturgical life should be allowed to become an obstacle to the ministry of souls. On the contrary, lived to the full, they would make the apostolic mission fruitful. The example of an evangelical life, lived in the concrete, would only serve to give added strength to the ministry of preaching.

Nevertheless the founder would not have been either very farsighted or realistic if he had wished to force his itinerant preachers to resemble monks whose vow of stability kept them within the security of monastery walls, to imitate canons attached to their cloisters. The reconciliation which he intended to effect in his Order would only be possible if a certain number of traditions were modified in his favor. Nor did Dominic hesitate for a moment to make these necessary changes.

Dispensations from this or that clause of the rule, until then, had been allowable only in case of sickness, but they could now be obtained by the preachers for reasons of study or the ministry, as well as those of health, because the Order had been founded for the salvation of souls and preaching.

Manual work was to be replaced by intellectual work: the primary duty of preachers was to instruct themselves "in the divine sciences." There were to be no fields to cultivate, no crops to gather, no lands to develop. The material poverty of the Order was to be for its members not only a means of imitating the Saviour and His Apostles, but a means whereby they could be "withdrawn from the care of temporal things, which may become an obstacle to the ministry of preaching." As for the divine office, it was to be sung "with dispatch and skill," so that the brethren "would not lose their sense of devotion and study would not suffer as a result."

It is true that Dominic knew what the spirit of his Order was to be when he took the road to Rome once more in October, 1216, but he had no idea as yet what the future renown and size of the Order were to be.

Innocent III was not the Pope who was destined to grant formal approbation to his Order. A few months after the Council of the Lateran, the Supreme Pontiff had died. But Honorius III, who succeeded him on the papal throne, granted the desired confirmation. Two important bulls, two memorable dates: December 22, 1216, January 21, 1217. Meanwhile, the founder went about Rome like a pilgrim and knelt at the tombs of the Apostles and martyrs, the earliest Christians, who, by their lives and deaths, had been like foundation stones for the Church of Christ. He made contact also with Roman circles, conversed with Cardinal Hugolin and conferred with the Pope himself.

The wave of evangelical fervor which had swept over northern Christendom ten years before was lapping at the walls of the Roman Curia itself. Bishops had arrived from the distant lands bordering the Baltic to inform Honorius III about the missions which were penetrating, farther and farther, into the areas toward the north and east. The harvest was immense, but the laborers were so few! Dominic was again greatly moved by what he heard. The passion for souls, which had prompted him on his return from Denmark to offer himself for the evangelization of those remote barbarians, was now burning in him more intensely than ever. He was now no longer a Canon of Osma—the latter title had been resigned—but was actually the father of the Order of Preachers. Why should he confine to a single diocese the apostolic activity of his brethren, his present and his future sons? Had not the Lord Jesus assigned the entire world to His Apostles to be converted? "Go, therefore, and make disciples of all nations."

As he was meditating and praying in the basilica of St. Peter, a wave of certainty swept over him, a vision perhaps. In any case, a mystical revelation, by which God Himself confirmed the founder in the true mission of his Order. He believed that he saw the Apostles Peter and Paul symbolically presenting him with the staff of a missionary of God and the book of truth: "Go and preach." "Then, as in a flash, he seemed to see his own sons spreading across the world, going out, two by two, to preach the Word of God to all peoples."

Henceforth there was no longer any doubt in the mind of Dominic, no further hesitation. His Order of Preachers was being called to an apostolate covering the entire world. It was from Rome, the center of the Church, and from its visible head that the Order was receiving its commission. Its role would not be merely to struggle against error, but to proclaim the truth of the Gospel everywhere and to all.

In the month of May, in this year of 1217, Dominic

again summoned all his brethren, those of Saint-Romain de Toulouse and those of Prouille, twenty in all at the most. He intended to reveal to them his great decision. As the Pope himself had said: "If the grain is allowed to remain heaped up it spoils; but if it is spread out it bears much fruit." So the new Friars Preachers would disperse throughout the world without further delay in order to devote themselves to their apostolic mission. His statement was heard with amazement by his brethren. There were even protests, and they did not come from the friars alone. In addition to the objections raised by certain persons, grave prelates felt called upon to utter their misgivings. The project was inane, a dangerous and even scandalous innovation. What founder of an order had ever dared to make such a proposal?

Dominic faced his opponents with complete serenity and humility. But he stuck boldly to his position. He replied to the bishops and abbots: "Do not oppose me, for I know what I am doing." To those who had become his sons by their profession, he said, in words marked both by an irrevocable firmness and a paternal gentleness: "Go with assurance, for the Lord will give you the gift of the divine word. He will be with you, and nothing will fail you."

Pierre Seila, nevertheless, felt that he would be unable to obey. How could he possibly bear the crushing burden of governing a convent? How could he bear the heavy burden of preaching so far away from

Dominic? The latter, however, was well aware of his personal limitations as well as his poverty: for baggage, the brother carried only a notebook in which were copied the homilies of St. Gregory. "Go, my son," the founder replied, "I will bring you with me to God. Never doubt this. You will win many to God and will bear much fruit."

Beside the hermitage of the Carceri at Assisi, there still stands the tree under which the Poverello traced a great sign of the cross on the ground and enjoined the birds to go and sing the praises of the Creator in the four corners of the world. This symbolic gesture of St. Francis was also performed by St. Dominic, his contemporary, on the feast of the Assumption in 1217. But it was the Preachers whom he was sending out in real life to the four corners of the world, to bring men the good news of the Gospel.

He knew, however, that among those whom he was sending out today, in very small groups, over the roads of Europe, on the roads of the entire world, tomorrow there would be weak men, inadequately trained even in the religious life. All fell far short of sharing his eagerness and his virtue! But what difference did it make? The Spirit was urging him to hasten the sowing. The future would show that he was right.

Two groups reached Paris, the capital of the university world and the center of theological thought: one under the leadership of Matthew of France, the other under the brother of Dominic, Mamès, who some time ago had come from Caleruega to join the team of Toulousan missionaries. Four brethren, among them Peter of Madrid, made their way to Spain. Three Provençaux remained in Toulouse. The two religious who were already in Prouille, sharing the sermons and the supervision of the nuns, would remain there. Two months later, Dominic himself, with one companion, set out for Rome. He must now devote himself to the gigantic tasks of completing the legislation for his Order and gaining its acceptance by the rest of Christendom, securing new recruits, and confirming—or rather reconfirming—the brethren in their vocations. On foot, as always, without money, he tirelessly made his way, covering unheard-of distances in less than three years. Bologna, Rome, Prouille and Toulouse, first of all. By the autumn of 1218 he was in New Castile, at Guadalajara, then in Madrid and Segovia. In May, 1219, he returned to the Narbonnaise, went on to Orléans and Paris by way of Rocamadour. In the summer of the same year he returned to Italy by way of Burgundy, the Jura, the shores of Lake Leman, crossed the Great St. Bernard, went down to Milan, then on to Piacenza, Parma, Modena, Bologna, and Florence. Again he must go to Rome, then to Viterbo, where the Curia had gone with Honorius III. Rome again, then Bologna, for the first general chapter which was to open on the vigil of Pentecost, May 17, 1220. The life of a founder had nothing of the "Golden Legend" about it, with miracles springing up like flowers under his feet. He was incessantly confronted by harsh reality: the tenacious prejudices of his age; the misunderstanding of diocesan authorities, who were unsympathetic or even hostile toward an innovation which upset the existing state of affairs, perhaps questionable in some respects, but which men of good will had nevertheless ended by accepting. He had to cope with the incessant quarrels arising from the overlapping of the temporal and spiritual powers in the Middle Ages; with the deficiencies and temptations of his own sons, not all of whom were of the stuff to keep up with him, according to his own pace, on the road toward heroic perfection; with the hostility, finally, of those who saw in him merely a determined adversary of heretics, any heretics, and whose lack of sympathy for his mission would pursue his memory long after his death.

The poverty which he expected of his companions was, in effect, an unheard-of thing. It was not only because it was arduous for a man to go all the way from Toulouse to Paris on foot, begging his bread on the way (in the manner of Benedict Joseph Labre), that John of Navarre rebelled and would set out only if he were given at least a little money! It was because the ideas of his Father Dominic—whom he nevertheless dearly loved and venerated—ran counter to the laws of the dioceses to which he was being sent. At Paris in 1213, at Rouen in 1214, it had been specifically decreed that every superior who authorized one of his religious to leave his convent "should furnish him with a sufficient number of horses and provisions, which were indispensable both for himself and his assistants." And the canon stated in precise terms the reason for the precept: "For it would be a disgrace to the Lord and to the class of religious, if the latter were compelled to beg."

If the chapter of Notre-Dame in Paris refused for months on end to authorize the first Friars Preachers to recite the divine office publicly in their chapel, or to celebrate Mass there, to hear confessions, or to preach, it was because reasons were not lacking for mistrusting itinerant preachers of this kind. The Cathari and Waldensians had been a terrible example of what could happen. It was also because the chapters and collegiate churches were anxious to assure their members "a standard of life in conformity with their dignity," a guise under which human nature, now and then, tended to reassert itself. To share the Mass stipends with these newcomers would further tend to diminish the income of every canon, curate, or parish priest. By what right was the Master of the Preachers presuming to demand from these men, who had nothing whatever to do with his Order, a sacrifice which the Church was not willing to impose on them?

Wherever he passed, therefore, Dominic started a kind of revolution by planting the leaven in the dough. Many a churchman was shocked by the poverty of his sons. Others were suspicious of the lack of enclosure or cloister. And who would ever have thought it proper, until then, for religious to frequent university courses, and even to make their own some of the chairs of philosophy? The truly revolutionary implications of such a step is in danger of escaping us today, just as a concrete image of the real structure of feudal Christendom escapes us. The latter was the very opposite of our modern civilization, distinguished by its official rejection of the transcendence and sovereignty of God, by the emancipation of individuals and nations, and by the triumph of technology and materialism.

6

The Order of Preachers: Early Growth

Although the difficulties encountered in those days by the founder of an evangelical and mendicant order were far different from those with which we are faced today in connection with the Christianization—or rather re-Christianization of the world—they were no less real or formidable. Yet his intuition proved to be more and more justified, farsighed, and timely. The ideal which he offered both to the students and masters of the universities of France, Spain, and Italy, and to the clerics whom he encountered on his continual wanderings, actually aroused in souls an echo of an unexpected depth. Scarcely had the new order been organized before vocations began to flow in.

At Rome he was successful in winning over the young Guillaume de Montferrat, a guest of Cardinal Hugolin, whom Dominic had got to know through his visits to the Cardinal. A friendship soon developed between them, based on mutual confidence. The founder imparted to the enthusiastic young man, who dreamed of following him to death, his own consuming ardor for the salvation of souls. Together they laid plans for the future; as soon as the Order of Preachers was well established, and, for his part, as soon as Guillaume had concluded his theological studies at Paris, both would leave to bring the good news of the Gospel to the pagans of the north. It was on this occasion that Dominic is supposed to have allowed his beard to grow, for a time at least, after the manner of missionaries. The pagans! Nothing could ever make him forget them. His great personal desire, now more than ever, was at last to be realized. Guillaume de Montferrat did not delay before assuming the habit of the Preachers.

A famous master, who for five years had held the chair of canon law at Paris and was dean of the collegiate church of Saint-Aignan d'Orléans was accompanying his own Bishop and a few priests en route to the Holy Land. In Rome the group intended to make a stopover to pass the Lenten season. Mature in age, endowed with rare qualities of mind and of heart,

Master Reginald nevertheless had, to a certain extent, grown to enjoy the comforts and privileges connected with the two titles of Doctor and Dean. But he remained unsatisfied. Hugolin spoke to him about Brother Dominic. He wished to hear the latter preach. He heard him. He never failed to attend any of his sermons, until the day when he was struck down by illness. The founder of the Preachers hastened to his bedside. A profound sympathy developed between the two men. Master Reginald had vainly allowed himself to be distracted, for a time, by an easy life, while in reality he held in his heart the ideal of the Preachers. He vowed to give himself to the Order. But the sickness worsened and his case became hopeless. It was then that "the Virgin Mary, the Queen of Heaven, the Mother of Mercy, appeared to him in visible form, while the fever was devouring him, and said, 'I anoint your feet with holy oil, so that they may be ready to proclaim the Gospel of Peace.'" Then she presented the dying man with the white habit and black mantle. Reginald at once got up, perfectly well and shaken to the depths of his soul. As soon as he had concluded his pilgrimage to the Holy Places, he gave himself completely to the Order; and Dominic did not hesitate to confer on him, at once, the responsibility for San Nicola in Bologna, before sending him on to Saint-Jacques in Paris.

Now Matthew of France, whom he found there, had regarded him formerly as "vain and dedicated to comforts." One day, unable to restrain himself any longer, he asked the former doctor of the University: "Do you not sometimes feel a profound repugnance rise up in you for this kind of life which is so different from the one you knew?" Reginald lowered his head. He was more embarrassed by the disclosure that he was about to make than by the memory of his past laxness: "I do not feel that I deserve to belong to this Order, for I find too much joy here." For Master Reginald, Dominic had more than mere esteem, he had real affection. He loved to tell the young students who crowded around him Reginald's story.

One day a bachelor of theology, fresh from the University of Paris, was filled with great enthusiasm by reason of the story that he had just heard. He was called Jordan, and he was from Saxony. Unable to restrain himself any longer, he confessed his thoughts to the founder and revealed his purpose of joining the Order. But Dominic knows that one must not go too fast in matters of divine grace. So he imposed a few months' delay on Jordan. The student could not but acquiesce in this decision. He resolved, however, to bring along with him to the convent of Saint-Jacques his friend Henry of Germany. The latter resisted at first, although the appeal of his comrade seemed to make more explicit an inner longing with which he had been struggling. "His reason told him that he ought to say yes; his indocile will drew him in the opposite direction." His soul torn, he went one night

85

to Notre-Dame de Paris to assist at matins. His struggle became a temptation to discouragement, if not to despair. "I see very well now, Blessed Virgin, that you are disdaining me. I shall have no place among the poor of Christ." Then suddenly he felt a great relief; peacefully and without reluctance he could pronounce his yes to God. With eyes still swollen from tears and heart overflowing with joy, he ran to his friend: "I have made my vow to the Lord and I shall fulfill it." "We put off until Lent the beginning of our noviciate," continues Jordan of Saxony. "That gave us time to win over Brother Léon, one of our comrades, who was later to be the successor of Brother Henry in the office of prior." Less than three years later, Jordan himself was to be the first successor of Dominic, as head of the Order of Preachers.

In truth, a kind of wave was sweeping over university circles in particular. One was no sooner won over to the Order than he did not cease until he, in turn, had won over others. In order to possess the precious pearls of the Gospel, it was too little to sell all that one had; should one not share with one's friends and one's neighbors the treasure without price which one has just discovered? As in the days of Bernard of Fontaine, who brought along with him to Clairvaux his brothers and his family, the appeal was going out to the young clerics studying at Paris and Bologna. And the convents of Saint-Jacques and San Nicola were beginning to be filled at an amazing rate.

Such a wave of vocations, however, was a cause of alarm to certain professors. Yet, even some of the masters themselves were being caught in the net. Witness Reginald of Orléans, who now preached so effectively at Bologna! Master Moneta of Cremona, a famous professor of the faculty of arts, had resolutely shut his ears to the appeal. His own pupils could see nothing except the Prior of San Nicola. "Master, if you would only listen to him! Master, come with us to the sermon!" "Go to the sermon?" Moneta protested. There was plenty of time! In fact, he had to admit that time was only his excuse; fear was the real reason for his refusal. Suppose that he himself were to be won over. Doubtless he could not prevent his students from running to the foot of the pulpit, even if he tried to. But he himself would not go, that was certain. Then came the feast of St. Stephen, a holiday. He had no excuse that day. And the students insisted: "Master, let us go to the sermon of Master Reginald." But he still wished to gain time: "Let us go to St. Procule first, to hear Mass." So they went to hear Mass, in fact two, then three Masses. The sermon will be over, Moneta thought to himself. "Master, let us go to the sermon," his students insisted. Finally he was obliged to give in. The cathedral was so crowded that they could not get in. The master thought that he had won at last, and from the porch they were standing, surrounded by the crowds, he heaved a sigh of relief. But the voice of the preacher was strong and Master Moneta could hear it. He heard and he trembled: "I behold the heavens open," cried Reginald; "yes, it is evident that the heavens are open today for those who would enter. Whoever wishes can come in, all doors are open. Let them consider and tremble, the poor negligent souls, who close their hearts and their mouths and their hands to God. Let them tremble, lest God close the kingdom of heaven to them and lest they be unable to enter. Why do you delay, my dear friends? The heavens are open!"

These words were enough for Master Moneta. Why delay any longer, closing his heart to the appeal of God? He went to find Brother Reginald. He admitted his reluctance, his fears, and his final resolve. On the spot he dedicated himself to the Order of Preachers. For one year, it is true, because of his responsibilities as a master of the faculty of arts, he would have to postpone his profession, but then he would be free and could assume the white woolen habit. But he was determined to employ this year fruitfully: "In compensation for the many people whom he had formerly kept away from the preaching of Reginald, he now brought many more not only to the sermon but to the Order itself."

Sometimes it happened that Dominic, moved by a sudden inspiration, took the lead and called this or that student to him by name and then conferred on him the habit of a Preacher with his own hands. Brother Etienne revealed, in the process of canonization, the unusual manner in which he had entered the Order. "When I was studying at Bologna, Master Dominic came there. He preached to the students and I confessed my sins to him. It seemed to me that he loved me. One evening as I was getting ready to have supper with my comrades, he sent two brethren to tell me: 'Dominic requests you to come to him immediately.'—'I will go after supper.'—'No,' they said, 'come at once.' So I got up, left everything, and went to him. I found him with many of the brethren in the convent of San Nicola. He said to the brethren: 'Show him how to make the *venia*' (a form of prostration used by the Dominicans when seeking admittance to the Order, or when receiving a command or a reproach from one's superior). When I had done it, I made my promise by a vow while kneeling at his feet. He clothed me with the habit of the Friars Preachers before I left. 'I wish to give you,' he said, 'the arms with which you are to fight the devil throughout the rest of your life.' I was greatly astonished and asked him by what impulse he had called me in this way, for I had never before spoken with him regarding my entrance into religion."

These are a few incidents and a few names culled from a large mass of material. But we must go on. After the joys, there were the rude deceptions, which sometimes upset the heart of the founder. In Germany there was the case of a prior who fled after being entrusted with the guardianship of a recently established monastery. Elsewhere an entire group of brethren renounced the life of poverty, to which they had believed themselves called. It should not be at all surprising that there were many recruits among the first vocations who were too weak to persevere. They were very few, however, and the chronicles mention a fact worth remembering: those religious who went away, in spite of the pressing exhortations of the founder, came back to him later, brought back to the Order by his silent prayer, his mortifications, his fasts, and his vigils.

Jordan of Saxony, who knew him personally in the course of these very years, has left us the following account: "He revealed himself at all times to be a man of the Gospel, both in word and deed. During the daytime no one was more joyous or sociable in mixing with friends or companions on the road. But at night, no one was more assiduous at keeping vigils, at prayer, and at offering all kinds of supplication. His days were shared with his neighbor, his nights with God." No matter how hard they looked or in whatever monastery, his early companions could never discover the cell of Master Dominic. But many had seen with their own eyes the penitential instrument of three iron chains with which he scourged himself every night. A concern for sinners the world over haunted him without ceasing, as at Osma, but with an ever greater intensity. And it was precisely in order that this supernatural compassion might be rendered efficacious, that he never shrank from any journey, any effort, any

labor, when there was question of increasing throughout the world the number of Preachers, who would be
as consumed as he was with zeal for the glory of God
and the salvation of men.

"Behold the ship of your Father Dominic," we read
in the *Dialogue* of St. Catherine of Siena, "and see
with what perfect order everything is arranged inside.
He wished his brethren to have no other thought than
My honor and the salvation of souls to be won through
the light of knowledge. It is this light which he wished
to make the principal objective of his Order."

The official approbation and letters of recommendation of the Supreme Pontiff himself, destined to ac-
credit throughout Christendom the Order of Preachers,
so novel in its objective and its organization, were in
the hands of the founder when the first Chapter
General convened at San Nicola in Bologna at Pentecost, 1220.

There could be no possible doubt on this score
in view of the papal bulls, which Master Dominic
now read to the assembled brethren. Just as a life of
monastic penitence, according to the age-old tradition
of the Church, was to be a source of personal sanctification for the monk, so the burden of fatigue and dangers
to which the Preachers were exposing themselves for
the salvation of others through preaching would be
their source of sanctification. The life of renunciation
which they embraced on the day of their profession was
no less real than that of the monks, for they had

resolved to carry out their functions as Preachers "in the lowliness of voluntary poverty." Moreover, they were not to question or interfere with any authority, whether in diocese or parish, any more than they were to expect to receive the least "returns" for their services. Their task was to be purely spiritual and to be pursued by purely spiritual means.

In truth, the very spirit of the Order inspired its organization. In the eyes of their first head, his sons would be men of the Gospel, who received their mandate from the Church, and whose constitutions would have no other aim than to allow them to respond to this vocation. How revealing in this regard are those texts compiled and promulgated by this first chapter of Bologna!

"The brethren who shall leave to preach, after having received the blessing, shall go forth and behave everywhere as men seeking their own salvation and that of their neighbors, in all perfect and with a truly religious spirit, as evangelical men, that is, men following in the footsteps of their Saviour. They shall speak to God or about God, with themselves or with neighbor. They must not receive or carry any gold, silver, money or gift, except for food, clothing, indispensable objects and books. . . .

"The superior should give the students the necessary dispensation so that they may not have to interrupt their studies or be hindered in them by duties or similar causes. If the master of studies considers it worthwhile, let there be reserved for them a special room where they can gather in his presence to discuss their doubts and their questions. . . . None of those who have been assigned to the ministry of preaching and study should receive any parish charge or temporal administration, in order that they may be able to fulfill the spiritual ministry which has been committed to them with greater liberty, unless, perchance, no other person can be found to fill the necessary posts. For it is not wrong for the brethren to be temporarily occupied by the needs of the day. . . .

"When on the road the Preachers and itinerants shall say their office to the extent of their ability and as best they can. They should be content with the office recited in the churches where they are staying for the time being."

It is difficult to say what is more admirable, the boldness of such legislation, or the freedom with which the founder insisted that it should be interpreted and applied, in concrete circumstances, by each superior.

"No one must have permission to change, add, or take anything away from these constitutions, at his own will. For if we become remiss about the least details, we must fear a gradual decline of the Order. Yet the superior shall have authority to dispense the brethren in his own convent whenever he thinks it necessary, principally as regards that which would interfere with study, preaching, or the profit of souls. For it must be recognized that our Order, from the first, has been instituted with a special view to preaching and the profit of souls, and our studies themselves should be directed principally and with the greatest ardor and strength, toward making us capable of being useful to the soul of our neighbor."

One could hardly be more explicit. Everything about the Order of Preachers was governed by this unique objective, namely, the salvation of souls, and directed toward concern for the universal redemption of mankind. In view of this unique passion for the glory of God—for the salvation of men makes sense only in this perspective—the search of the religious for personal perfection becomes, to a certain extent at least, a secondary matter. For St. Benedict and St. Bernard, to fail to observe a precept of the monastic rule which the monk had sworn to observe by vows of religion, constituted a fault, a very grave fault, under certain circumstances. Dominic wished nothing of the sort for his sons and his daughters. He wished the rules to be subordinate to the end that it was intended to serve, and to be capable, therefore, of being modified at times when some apostolic necessity required. The rules imposed on his Order were not to be binding, in themselves, under pain of sin. He willingly admitted that one could derogate from them, without fault. These rules were only to be a means—one of great importance, no doubt!—a means and not an end, for those whose complete ideal it would be to "live as apostolic men, by following in the footsteps of their Saviour."

Now certain disputes were bound to arise among the brethren with regard to the interpretation of this point, and fears were expressed that the religious life itself would be threatened by adherence to such a novel ideal. But the founder maintained his position. "If he thought that some brethren were of another mind, he would go through the convents," he assured them, "and with his own hands would efface the rules by scratching them out with his own knife." The saints are sometimes bold in a way that is disconcerting; this is because they know better than we do what the demands of God's love are toward those whom He loves, and the genuine liberty of those who suffer themselves to be moved by the Spirit because they are the "true sons of God."

"A truly royal discipline," commented St. Catherine of Siena, "a truly broad-minded, joyous, perfumed religion; a veritable garden of delights." It was, indeed. For in spite of the note of austerity as well as the penitential side of the Order, from the first there was an element of joyous gladness and the suggestion of an amazingly youthful soul about it, which is still breathed forth by the old documents, signed with the seal and oath of the first generation of the brethren.

7

Dominic the Man

"Full of zeal for the observance of the rule,
Brother Dominic would severely punish faults," notes
Ventura of Verona, "but he inflicted penances with
such gentleness and kindness, that the brethren accepted them willingly." Brother Rudolph says in particular: "He was merciful and kind toward his brethren.
If he saw anyone commit a fault, he pretended that he
had seen nothing. Then, later, he would go to that
person calmly and say to him gently: 'Brother, you have
done wrong, admit it.' His words, so full of kindness,
induced them all to confess their faults and do pen-

ance. He meticulously punished their transgressions, but the humility with which he spoke to them caused them to feel consoled afterwards." And there is the anonymous statement, so fresh and appealing: "One would almost have transgressed the rule voluntarily in order to receive afterward such wonderful correction."

However, the confidence which Dominic displayed toward all, even the humblest of his brethren, did not affect the clearsightedness which told him to be on guard against human frailty, even among the best of the brethren. If the rule and the constitutions of the Order did not oblige under pain of sin, those who transgressed them knew that they must submit, with good heart, to the merited penance, and to the decisions of their superior, according to a penal code applied in the Chapter of Faults. For the brethren were obliged to accuse themselves, publicly, in the presence of the community, of their external faults. And all would regard it as a duty of the highest fraternal charity to point out in this same chapter the failings of which their brethren had omitted to accuse themselves. Thus they became themselves the guardians of the rule, which, in the last resort, had no other purpose than to help them to free themselves from whatever would be an obstacle on the road they were striving to follow, namely to "follow in the footsteps of the Saviour."

In this, moreover, as in every other respect, the founder himself set the example. At the opening of the chapter of Bologna he accused himself in all humility of not having accomplished as perfectly as ought to have been expected, the charge with which he had been invested: "I deserve to be deposed," he said, before all the assembled brethren, "for I am useless and remiss." A manifest exaggeration, we are inclined to think, which was so obviously contradicted by the facts. But in the light of the transcendence of God and of His infinite holiness, the saints sometimes have reactions which seem absurd to us, because they are beyond our comprehension. It is they, however, who are right; we have no right to doubt this.

"Brother Dominic," Brother Rudolph also declared later, observed the rule and customs of the Friars Preachers even to the minutest details, both in what applied to him as well as to others, in clothing, food and drink, fasts and rest. . . . He always assisted at the divine office, always followed the community, whether to choir or the table. . . . When bread or any other food or wine was lacking to the monastery, the procurator— and this was brother Rudolph himself—went to find Brother Dominic and said to him: 'We have no bread,' or 'no wine.' He would then reply to him: 'Go and pray, and the Lord will provide for us.' So he went to pray in the church, often followed by Brother Dominic, and God always arranged that they had the necessary nourishment. Sometimes at Dominic's bidding the brother put on the table the little bread that they had and the Lord made up for what was lacking. Then, as if he were afraid that his deposition would be questioned, brother Rudolph added: 'The witness knows all this because he lived with Brother Dominic and very often saw that which he has just described.' "

From Brother Buonviso, who also was procurator in the convent of Bologna, we also have a precious account: "One certain fast day, the bread failed. Brother Dominic made a sign to place it before the brethren. The brother told him there was none. Then, calmly and with radiant face, he raised his hands, praised the Lord and gave thanks to Him. At the same instant there entered two young men carrying baskets, the one full of bread, the other of dried figs, so that the brethren had what they needed to eat in abundance. The brother knows this because he was a witness of it."

One never fails to mention, in this connection, the exquisite scene depicted by Fra Angelico, known under the name of the "Miracle of Angels." The silent, restful, and devout atmosphere of the conventional refectory, its poor, simple furnishings, the arrangement of the tables, the raised chair for the reader, the *nola* or little bell that the prior shakes when the brethren, two by two, enter in procession, in the "ceremony of silence," nothing has escaped the attention of this son of Dominic, whose real name John of Fiesole. The art here is not merely symbolical, but an accurate rendering of reality. Everything, even the simplest details, is intended to provide us with an authentic "image" of Dominican life, as it was handed down since the first chapter of Bologna. Such as it has come down to us, after more than seven hundred years.

Therefore when the chapter meeting had ended in May, 1220, Dominic—who henceforth bore the official title of *Magister Ordinis Praedicatorum*—renewed the gesture by which, the day after the Assumption in 1217, he had sent forth his earliest disciples into the world. "If the grain is allowed to remain heaped up it will spoil; but if it is spread out it will bear much fruit." They were then twenty; they are now several hundred. The following year they would already be divided into five provinces: Spain, Provence, France, Lombardy, and Rome. They leave from the convent of San Nicola, wearing the tunic and scapular of white wool—the ordinary dress of the day—their shoulders covered by the black cape and hood, as we can see from one of the sculptures on the cathedral of Osma. They go forth over the roads of Europe, whether to convents already established, or to prepare new foundations which will spring up everywhere in the succeeding months.

Dominic, too, takes up his staff. By command of Honorius III he must traverse the roads of northern Italy. He must assume, in addition to his cares and responsibilities as founder, the direction of a new apostolic mission in Lombardy. The latter was a repetition, to some extent, of the Narbonnaise mission, but with the difference that, whereas he had formerly been merely the least of a group, Dominic was now destined to have complete responsibility for the new venture, even over religious who did not belong to his Order, and whom the Pope had expressly ordered to take part in the new preaching mission. The errors to be unmasked were apparently the same in northern Italy as in southern France. Virtually identical also were the vices of the faithful. Here, as there, numerous political rivalries were at work, the cause of so much brutality and endless violence, and the same poisoned atmosphere of doctrinal dispute. City was ranged against city, family against family. Accusations were rife and reputations were impugned. It was in such an atmosphere of excitement, hatred, and vengeance that Dominic was called upon to proclaim the Gospel of peace. It was a delicate, a crushing task, which called for all the strength the Father of the Preachers could muster.

At Milan where he laid the foundations for a new house, he fell seriously ill, suffering from an acute attack of dysentery. This was the third time in a year that he had succumbed to illness. Once again, very soon, he revived and was well. We know from his traveling companions the indomitable energy he often displayed under such circumstances. "Very often he was a prey to great pains," notes Constantine of Orvieto; "his companions would then place him on a bed. But I saw him get up at once and lie on the ground, for it was not his custom to lie in bed."

Brother Paul of Venice "who, for more than two years accompanied him through practically the whole of the March of Treviso, shared his meals, drinking, stopping, walking, and reciting the office with him day and night," makes the following statement: "I do not remember ever having heard Master Dominic utter a useless, slighting, flattering, or mean word. On the contrary, when we were traveling together, I saw him pray, preach, and devote himself to meditation. He would say to those accompanying him: 'Go on ahead, so that we can think for a while about the Saviour.' Then they would hear him groan and sigh. Wherever he happened to be, he spoke without ceasing of God or with God, and he exhorted his brethren to do the same. And he wrote this in the constitution of the Friars Preachers. . . . One day, in the village of Dugliolo, when he was asking for alms, a man gave him a whole loaf of bread. The father received the gift on his knees, with great humility and devotion. The witness often heard him tell the brethren that they should live by alms. When traveling with him, the brethren never saw him lie down in a bed: he would lie down in the straw but rarely. . . . He fasted while he was on the road, but he made those who were accompanying him eat, because of the fatigue of the journey."

Accounts such as this have the ring of truth about them. It is not difficult to imagine the tiresome stretches of road, the chance stops, the lack of food, the hunger, the thirst, the overpowering weariness, or the rain which soaked their heavy mantles, the sharp stones which tore their aching feet. When he was passing through the countryside, in order not to be confused with the heretic preachers, and also for reasons of poverty and mortification, Dominic removed the sandals which he had adopted for himself and his brethren. He always tried to engage in conversation with the travelers he chanced to meet, to the extent that his knowledge of the language of the country permitted, for he wished to awaken in the souls of all a sense of God. He often spoke with his brethren, but always on the same subject, God and the redemption of the world. Or again, alone, a little apart from the rest, he would pray in silence. At other times he was heard chanting aloud the verses of the "Veni Creator" or the "Ave Maris Stella."

8

In the Family of Dominic

When Dominic once again passed through the gates of Rome toward the end of 1220, people were still talking about the splendid ceremonies, in November, in connection with the coronation of Frederick II, the ruler of the Holy Roman Empire. It had been a significant event, if we bear in mind the intermittent conflict that had gone on years between the powers of the Empire and of the Papacy. The Master of the Preachers, however, had not been summoned back to contemplate these splendors. He had come back for quite different reasons.

He was to give Honorius III an account of the Lombard mission, to which he had been devoting all his energies since the previous spring. He must take care of many details, at the Curia, regarding the dispersal of his Preachers throughout Christendom. Finally, a new task was assigned to him by will of the Supreme Pontiff, that of founding at San Sisto a convent of nuns belonging to his Order. The project went back to the time of Innocent III, but his successor was now prepared to take it up. The time had come to realize it. Many convents of women were in a deplorable state at the beginning of the thirteenth century, a fact that greatly disturbed the Papacy, especially regarding those in Rome itself. Political rivalries, incessant wars, epidemics, and many other external causes, to mention only the latter, had brought great harm, if not ruin, to the houses of women religious in Italy. Energetic measures were necessary if this tendency toward decline were to be reversed.

The Pope had already restored the church of San Sisto the Old, on the Via Appia opposite the Baths of Caracalla, with a view to establishing in Rome itself a genuinely regular convent of women, to which could be assigned the nuns from various communities now no longer flourishing. The word "restore" is perhaps not strictly accurate. The old fifth century basilica had literally fallen in and been buried. According to the customs of the time, the architects did not try to resurrect the primitive church, but used its walls as the foundation for a new structure. Church and monastery had been granted to Master Dominic in December, 1219, on condition that he and his brethren would assume responsibility for the establishment and spiritual direction of the nuns there. At Christmas of the same year the Preachers had taken possession of the existing buildings. The construction of quarters for the religious had gone on, not without arousing the curiosity of the Romans.

This was because two remarkable events had occurred in connection with the work, which had been the topic of conversation throughout the Eternal City. A Roman, one Jacopo de Melle, a member of the Order, had been appointed procurator of the new community. In the latter capacity he was obliged to look after the building operations, when suddenly he became so seriously ill that he had to receive the last sacraments. The brethren were already gathering for the prayers for the recommendation of his soul to God. The outlook was bleak. Then Dominic, still hopeful when others had given up hope, succeeded in obtaining the man's complete and immediate recovery by his prayers.

Even more spectacular was the second miracle, which had to do with a terrible accident involving the building operations themselves. A portion of the ancient walls collapsed, burying as in a cave in a part of the primitive church an architect whom the brethren had hired. When the brethren and workmen succeeded in removing the rubble, a man appeared to be dead. Despair swept over the community. No sooner had

Dominic, learning of the disaster, appeared on the scene, than the architect regained consciousness and stood up, as if nothing at all had happened.

How could the Romans have failed to be attached to the convent of San Sisto, the scene of such remarkable events? By the beginning of 1221, when the work of construction was almost complete, a number of young Roman women had decided to consecrate themselves to God in the new community, which was to be under the administration and spiritual direction of the new Friars Preachers. Some of the sisters of Santa Bibiana were also preparing to join, but the Benedictine nuns of Santa Maria *in Tempulo* were the ones whom the Pope especially had in view in pursuing his plans for reform. However, for at last a year, ever since they had learned of the intended reform, the latter had been firmly and bluntly opposed to the move. Their families, in particular, were resolutely against the prospect of an absolute enclosure. Although it would mean an infringement of existing, recognized rights, the Pope maintained that the step was necessary to restore discipline. In view of such widespread laxity, a strict enclosure seemed to be the only way to assure the observance of a genuinely religious life.

The return of Dominic to Rome naturally aroused past fears. The fear of imminent enclosure spread to the Roman nobility, whose daughters were religious in Santa Maria *in Tempulo*. Honorius III even had to call upon certain cardinals who came from these families to exert their influence. The Pope had been compelled by circumstances to ask the nuns to sacrifice their semienclosure, which was their right according to the privileges of their order, and to give up, also, their Benedictine rule. Moreover, the buildings of Santa Maria were falling into ruin and the Abbess now found herself unable to meet the financial demands of her creditors. Brother Dominic was nonetheless in an extremely delicate position in relation to the nuns who were being sent, against their will, from one monastery to another, from one rule to another. He hoped, naturally, to induce them to understand the sacrifice which was being demanded of them by the highest authority on earth, that of the Vicar of Jesus Christ, whose aim was sufficiently lofty to justify even the most painful and disagreeable renunciation.

For weeks, months, perhaps, he went to the half-ruined monastery, speaking to the sisters and hearing their confessions; he won over several of their number, including the abbess, who was very advanced in years. Were it not for the unyielding, noisy opposition of the families, the cause would doubtless have been won without a struggle. But the families, who had themselves not taken the vow of obedience, would not desist. On Ash Wednesday (the 24th of February), 1220, the Master of the Preachers summoned the nuns of Santa Maria to San Sisto for the beginning of Lent. There was a great feeling of relief after the instruction which he gave them in the church. All, with the exception of one, resolved to make their profession before him, to enter the cloister and never again to go outside, unless he should think it advisable. The abbess herself officially resigned her title as well as her authority. Eight nuns of Prouille were expected any moment in Rome and would initiate the Roman religious in their new duties, rules, and customs. The nuns of Santa Maria made only one stipulation as the price for their transfer and complete enclosure: the venerated ikon of the Mother of God, which they kept in their monastery, must follow them to San Sisto. It was a famous image, very much beloved by the Roman people. Once, when it had been transferred to the Lateran, on the orders of Pope Sergius III, it is supposed to have returned miraculously to Santa Maria. Obviously, therefore, if the holy image did not wish to remain at San Sisto and returned to the monastery which had formerly housed it, the nuns would have to be free to consider themselves released from their vows. Dominic agreed to this condition and the sisters returned, provisionally, to Santa Maria, until the convent of San Sisto would be ready to receive them. Unfortunately the delay enabled the storm of protests to break forth in the city again. Some of the sisters felt themselves weakening in their resolve. Alerted, Dominic arrived at once. He ordered all the doors closed and the keys given over to him, while the outside was to be guarded day and night by convert brethren. These precautionary measures were not uncalled for. A few months hence, Diana d'Andalo, spiritual daughter of the Master of the Preachers to whom she had given her promise to consecrate herself to God, would be forcibly snatched by her own family from the monastery of Ronzano, near Florence, where she had fled. She had determined to don the habit of an Augustinian while awaiting the time when she could make her profession as a Dominican in a new convent which Dominic was establishing in Bologna. The uproar was so intense, the methods used so brutal, that the young girl was brought back to her father's house with a broken rib. This made no difference, however! Her parents were implacable and kept her hidden from view for an entire year.

Moreover, Diana's case was not an isolated one. Such were the customs of the times. The use of force was felt to be perfectly justified in such cases, an attitude that would hardly be condoned today.

The authority exercised by Dominic in causing the nuns of Santa Maria to be kept under strict enclosure while awaiting transfer to San Sisto had the effect of throwing cold water on further attempts at rebellion. From then on both the ouside and the inside of the grills were kept guarded. But, under these conditions, it was desirable that the transfer should take place as soon as possible. The buildings were now sufficiently ready to be able to receive the forty religious from Santa Maria, the sisters of Santa Bibiana, and the eight nuns from Prouille—almost seventy religious in all, a fact which explains the building which had been going on. But the buildings were still occupied, in part, by a community of Preachers, whom Honorius III was anxious to establish in Rome. Was the question of housing now going to compromise the reform of the nuns in Rome at the last moment? Dominic hoped that this would not be the case. Not without considerable trouble, he obtained from the Pope the latter's family fortress on the top of the Aventine and the basilica of Santa Sabina incorporated in it, both dating from the fifth century. As soon as this gift had been acquired, the brethren vacated their quarters on the Via Appia. A few days after Easter, in the month of April, Dominic was finally able to make the monastery of San Sisto available to the nuns. Standing on the threshold of the church, he greeted the Benedictines from Santa Maria. They were garbed at once in the robes and scapular of white wool and black veil which were worn by the sisters of Prouille and Madrid. Each one renewed her profession and promise of obedience before him, in conformity with the rule and institutions which Dominic now gave them. In the course of the same day the sisters of Santa Bibiana and the others who came individually from various houses in the city, as well as a number of postulants, received their habits from his hands. Then, when evening had come, the Master of the Preachers, accompanied by two cardinals, went in solemn procession to Santa Maria to bring back the ikon of the Blessed Virgin. Barefoot and carrying torches they brought the ikon to its new home, escorted by a procession of the brethren and their friends. The sisters, barefoot also, awaited it at San Sisto, and after greeting it, placed it with great reverence in the new monastery. "It is there today," observes Sister Caecilia, not without a note of triumph, at the end of her long life. She was only eighteen years old in Easter 1221.

One fact also must be mentioned in concluding this story, a fact that is historically certain and not merely an anecdote, which underscores the divine approbation for the work of San Sisto. We owe it to the pen of Jordan and shall repeat it here just as he set it down. "A certain young man, a relative of Cardinal Fossanova"—one of those who took part in the nocturnal procession—"amused himself by taking part in a wild horse race and suffered a great fall. He seemed to be half-dead, perhaps altogether dead. In any case he was unconscious. Everyone was in despair. Master Dominic arrived. Brother Tancred was with him, the fervent and good brother who was Prior of Rome, and who told me this story. 'Why are you stealing away?' he said to Dominic. 'Why do you not call on the Lord? Where is your famous compassion for your neighbor? Where is your complete confidence in God?' Much affected by these remarks of his brother, and at the same time feeling a wave of compassion for the young man, he caused the latter to be carried into a room which was locked behind him, and then, by means of his prayers, restored him to life and brought him out, safe and sound, be-

fore all." The incident took place right in front of the
convent of San Sisto, and at about the time when the
sisters of Santa Maria came here, for the first time, at
the beginning of Lent.

The story of the nuns of Rome is an original one.
Yet the firmness and decision then shown toward them
by Brother Dominic, as on other occasions, should not
be allowed to blur his true image. Those who knew
him most intimately, both men and women, have declared, not once but often, how gifted he was in the
spiritual direction of women religious. He was strict,
of course, but his guidance went right to the point, as
we can see from the letter which he sent to the nuns
of Madrid in 1218. It is the only part of the correspond-
ence of the Master of the Preachers which has come
down to us! But was this strictness not a sign of his
great love and confidence? How often he would
descend from Santa Sabina to San Sisto, in order to
give the best of himself to his daughters, to encourage
them in their vocations, and to associate them with the
apostolate of his brethren! He did so, because, in his
own words, "they had no other master to train them
for the life of the Order."

We must include here, without altering a single
word, the account which we owe to Sister Caecilia. "He
came one evening later than was his custom. So the
sisters, thinking that he would not come, had left the
chapel and gone to the dormitory. Suddenly the
brothers sounded the little bell which served as a
signal for the sisters to gather when the blessed father

came to visit them. Hearing this, all the sisters came in haste to the church, they opened the gate and found him already seated with the brothers awaiting them. He said to them: 'My daughters, I have come from fishing and the Lord has given me a great fish.' He was referring to Brother Gaudio, an only son of a certain Lord Alexander, a noble Roman. He then delivered a very moving instruction and revealed that he was filled with consolation. After the discussion he said: 'It would be good, my sons, if we had some refreshment.' He called Brother Roger, the cellarer, and told him to bring a cup. The brother brought what was asked of him, and blessed Dominic ordered him to fill the cup to its brim. Then he blessed it, first drank himself, and then gave it to all the brethren present. And when the brethren had all drunk, the blessed Dominic said: 'Now I wish that all my daughters should drink too.' Calling Sister Nubia, he said: 'Go, take the cup, and give it to all the sisters to drink.' So she went with a companion and took the cup, full to the brim, and even though it was so full not a drop was spilled. Then all the sisters drank, beginning with the prioress, as much as they wished. And the blessed father kept saying to them: 'Drink at your ease, my daughters.' "

If we can believe Sister Caecilia, the cup was never emptied until the last of the sisters had drunk. The miracle is possible, and interesting. More so, however, the engaging simplicity of the scene, like that of a "family gathering."

9

The Final Legacy

In fact, it was as "one family" that Brother Dominic was now going to leave the two first branches of his Order. Brothers and sisters were vowed ultimately to the same apostolate. One did so by preaching, the fruit of contemplation; the other by a life of penitence and prayer, by means of which they also carried on just as effectively the work of the salvation of souls.

There would come a day when the Church would entrust to the sisters new tasks of an apostolic nature permitting them, also, to hand on the divine truth, in accordance with the needs of a new age. The Third Order of Dominican sisters would then find its place in the Order of Friars Preachers. And these authentic daughters of St. Dominic know that they are following exactly in the line which he laid down himself seven hundred years ago.

It is remarkable that, when speaking of this man of such prodigious energy, forcefulness, and unconquerable zeal, one of the greatest builders of his time—perhaps of all time—those who knew him best constantly used the word "meekness" with reference to him. This meekness, of course, was not softness, but the kind of meekness which our Lord meant in the Sermon on the Mount, when He called the meek blessed, or when spoke of Himself as "meek and humble of heart." The word "consolation" is also found closely associated with him. Let us choose, at random, some of the phrases which appear in the canonization process: "Brother Dominic was joyous, patient, and merciful, full of kindness and consoling to the brethren. . . ." "He was very even-tempered, patient, kind, and very merciful, easy to talk to and just. . . ." "The brethren never had any better or greater consoler." "I know this well," Brother Etienne said, "because when I was at the beginning of my religious life, when I was still a novice, temptations of all sorts assailed me all at once. And I was completely consoled by the advice and preaching of Dominic. And I have heard many of the brethren say that they also had experienced the same consolation." What can we say in the face of such overwhelming evidence?

No text or sermon notes has been preserved for us by the earliest sons of one who was the founder of an Order expressly devoted to preaching. St. Bernard, the reformer of a cloistered, monastic order, has left us almost three hundred.

Breaking with the centuries-old tradition of the Church, Dominic planted his convents in the very midst of society, in the center of towns, especially university towns. His earliest companions are unanimous in reporting of him, that he "spoke only with God or about God."

He was the first also who wished his brethren to frequent the universities. At first, he accompanied them himself when they went to hear the courses of Master Tavensby at Toulouse. When toward the end of his life one of the young brothers, studying at Bologna, asked him in what book he had studied the most, he replied as follows: "In the book of charity, more than in the books of men."

No portrait was made of the Father of the Preachers during his lifetime. The only information that we have in this regard is the description which Sister Caecilia has left us, a portrait engraved on her heart and which she tried to express in words more than a half a century after the death of the saint. Obviously her words were the source of inspiration for the Dominican painters and miniaturists of the thirteenth and fourteenth centuries.

The miniatures found in the work entitled "The

Nine Manners of Prayer of St. Dominic" seem to date from approximately fifty years after his canonization. The masterpieces of Fra Angelico date from a century and a half later. But there can be no doubt both that in both cases we are in the presence of an authentic witness. It was the soul of their blessed Father, his spirit, if we may say so, which his sons were trying to express in their pictures. This was the spirit which continued in the life of the Order and which they hoped to exemplify in their own lives.

The text compiled—and doubtless also illustrated —during the lifetime of brethren who had known the Master of the Preachers, entitled "The Nine Manners of Prayer of St. Dominic," and not, be it noted, "The Nine Manners of Preaching" (which we might have perhaps expected), is not without significance in this respect. At first sight the treatment appears to be largely conventional, then we are impressed by the detail in each miniature, which provides us with a key to the whole series.

Whether Dominic is represented as "humbly prostrate before the altar—stretched out praying with his face on the ground—kneeling and stripped to the waist, flagellating himself with a rude discipline—genuflecting repeatedly—standing with his hands in front of his breast in the form of an open book—with his arms stretched out in the form of a cross—with hands raised toward heaven like an arrow—seated, quietly reading a book open before him—or with his face buried in his hands, shedding abundant tears," the artist always is careful to place a crucifix in front of his blessed father. And from the breast of Christ there is always a stream of water and blood which gushes forth like a spring. There seems to be a deliberate intention to recall the verse of St. John[13] as well as the words of the Paschal Liturgy like the evocation of a musical theme repeated over and over again until it hypnotizes the hearer.

"Et continuo exivit sanguis, et aqua . . ."
"Vidi aquam egredientem a latere dextro . . ."
"Immediately there came out blood and water . . ."
"I saw water coming from his side . . .
    and all those whom this water reaches were saved."

This is the very theme which Fra Angelico will take up later and attempt to portray in an even more realistic manner. In his canvases and frescoes, Dominic no longer stands merely before a crucifix, but, like John and Magdalen, he is at the foot of the cross, sometimes alone, sometimes beside Mary and the "disciple whom Jesus loved." It is amazing how often in the cells of San Marco at Florence we find ourselves before the Crucifixion scene.

But it is the cloister fresco, above all, which is the most evocative. Dominic is portrayed on his knees, at the foot of the cross, his hands holding the wood, fascinated by Christ. Blood flows from the latter's hands and His feet and gushes from His open side. The infinite price of the incomprehensible love of a God, offering His life for the love of those who offend Him, offering eternal salvation to all, the life of union and intimacy with the Father, the Son, and Holy Spirit. But for some this great sacrifice will remain in vain. There are men who do not wish to be saved. Dominic is aware of this. That is his special grace. That is the drama of his life. Truth and Love unknown. "What is to become of sinners?" Unspeakable compassion of a human heart, with which the heart of Christ wished to share its own compassion! Real compassion which causes Dominic to desire to know all that Christ has suffered for the redemption of the world, and "to make up in his own flesh that which is lacking in his passion."

Anguished lover, total oblation of himself in complete confidence, all this can be read on the face of Dominic, who reaches out in fervent, silent prayer toward the Lord Jesus, hanging on the cross. In the face of such reality as this everything else fades into insignificance for him. What are sufferings, struggles, fatigues, insults compared with the love of the Son of God dying for the salvation of the world?

The whole Dominic is there, contemplation and apostolic action, which with him are one and the same. He could not separate them, for it was the life of Christ which he aspired to reproduce, *usque ad mortem,* even to death. Christ was his model, his only model. It was not to be otherwise for his sons or his daughters.

This, no doubt, is what explains those contrasts between a life that was so austere, yet at the same time so fruitful and profitable. As the bull of canonization dated July 3, 1234, was to put it, issued by his friend Cardinal Hugolin, who became Pope under the name of Gregory IX:

"Dominic is the intrepid athlete, who followed with fidelity the paths of justice and the way of the Saints. He who never abandoned, even for a moment, the tabernacle of the Lord, with perfect balance, devoted himself wholeheartedly to works of mercy. He who gave himself entirely to the word of God, by preaching the Gospel, because zeal for the salvation of souls caused him to feel an inexpressible joy. He who engendered a great many sons, and deserved therefore on earth the name and dignity of patriarch."

Pope Gregory IX had the unique experience of being able to enroll in the catalog of saints a friend whom he had known, loved, and cherished for many years, and he could not refrain from inserting in his bull of canonization the following personal reminiscence and wish: "We believe that after having consoled us on earth by his friendship, so full of warmth, he will grant us the joy of his powerful patronage in heaven." Then the Pope added these words, which are so meaningful with reference to the official neglect of the memory of Dominic by his later sons: "In him I have known a man who observed the rule of the Apostles in its entirety, and I have no doubt that he will be associated with their glory in heaven."

After the translation of the sisters to San Sisto, Dominic returned to Rome for the second chapter general of his Order. It was Pentecost, 1221. Nothing new took place in this second plenary reunion of the representatives of the Order, merely a determination to continue along the lines which had been firmly laid down the year before.

Then again the brethren dispersed. Brother Dominic himself left for Venice. He had been ordered by Honorius III to join Cardinal Hugolin there and help him with the mission of preaching. He must have reached there by June.

The news about Diana d'Andalo and her virtual incarceration reached the ears of the Master of the Preachers in the course of the following months. He went on to Bologna, but took advantage of stops to go on with his ministry. The heat was overpowering, and the climate of the Po Valley extremely unhealthy. When he reached San Nicola, he had come to the end of his strength. Exhaustion, cares, fever, anxiety over the fate of Diana, one of his dearest spiritual daughters, all weighed heavily on his worn-out body. It was evening. The prior of the convent tried to persuade Dominic to get some rest, before doing anything else. But there were so many important and pressing matters to take care of! He must begin with what he regarded as the primary concern of the Order, the salvation of souls. The hours passed, the hour of rest had long ago sounded for the other brethren. Timidly Brother

Rudolph, the procurator, who very much wanted to sleep himself and who was very alarmed by the changed expression on his father's face, begged him to go and get a little rest, and to lie down until the morning, dispensing himself for once for matins. But Dominic did not think that he should give in. Since he was now in the house, he thought it better for him to be present at the office over which he had so often presided, going from one choir to the other exhorting his brethren to chant the psalms with greater love. He went to the church and knelt down in silent prayer, as his custom was, waiting for the matins bell to ring in the night. But after the office the brethren went to warn the prior. "Master Dominic is suffering from a terrible headache."

By another supreme effort of will he succeeded in dominating the malady for a few more days. With Cardinal Hugolin, he went to visit the father of Diana d'Andalo. He could see his spiritual daughter, but not speak to her. Then, knowing that his days were numbered, he began to visit the cells of each of the youngest of the brethren who were studying in Bologna.

Finally he was obliged to give up and consented to lie down, for the first time, on a woolen mattress placed on a simple wooden frame. He was suffering but he did not complain. Instead, he prayed. If he could no longer speak to men about God, he would now speak to God about men. Calm and smiling, he received the brethren who came to him. He even asked that they bring him the novices. With them he could still talk, simply and without pretense, about God, the Order, and redemption.

His brothers could not bring themselves to admit that he was going to leave. He was scarcely fifty years old. They felt that the convent of San Nicola, so near the river Aposa and the stagnant waters of the moat, was not the best place to care for one so seriously ill. On the top of the hill of Monte Mario there was a little Benedictine priory. The monks there gladly offered its hospitality to the Master of the Preachers. The air was cerainly much better and lighter than at San Nicola. Brother Dominic submitted to the desire of his brethren and allowed himself to be carried there.

By the dawn of August 6th everyone had to admit that the end was near. Brother Ventura, the prior, came with about twenty religious. The Master of the Preachers wished to impart his last wishes to his sons and daughters of today, tomorrow, and always. Brother Ventura informs us that he spoke with such moving words that they had never heard the like before. Why then, Father Prior, has no one thought to preserve them for posterity? Tradition tells us that he spoke of the love of souls, holiness, poverty, and perseverance, but the words themselves have not come down to us.

Dominic asked for Extreme Unction. The rite was nearly completed, when suddenly one of the brethren who had entered whispered something to the Prior. He had just learned that if their father was to die at Monte Mario, the Benedictines intended to keep in their own monastery the mortal remains of the Father of the Preachers. The brethren were very excited at the news. Brother Ventura explained to the dying man what he had just heard. "God be pleased that I may never be buried anywhere except under the feet of my brethren. Transfer me away from here. If I should die on the road, you can then bury me in your church!"

So the brethren at once took up the bier on which the dying man was lying. With slow tread they made their way down the hillside. They reached San Nicola. They carried the father into the cell of Master Moneta, for he had none of his own. A brief interval followed in which the brothers approached their father one by one. But they were no longer unable to restrain their tears, and Dominic, for one last time, was again moved by their suffering: "Do not weep! I will be more useful to you and will bring you more fruit after my death than I did in my life."

An hour went by in silence. Then the dying man called Brother Ventura: "Prepare yourselves." The prior leaned over him: "Father, you know how sad we are that you are leaving us. Remember us and pray to the Lord for us." Then the dying man, raising his hands to heaven, repeated the words of the prayer of Christ the evening of the Last Supper: "Holy Father, you know that I followed your will with my whole heart. And I have preserved and guarded those whom

125

you have given to me. I recommend them to you. Preserve them and guard them."

Brother Rudolph, kneeling, supported the head of the dying man with a cloth. "Begin," murmured Dominic. Together the brethren began to recite the Creed. They then began the moving prayers for the recommendation of a departing soul. ". . . Come to his aid, O saints of God; attend, all angels of God. Receive his soul and offer it in the sight of the Most High."

A hardly noticeable raising of the hands toward heaven. At this precise moment Brother Dominic gave his last sigh. It was the 6th of August, 1221. Night was falling.

Was not this the hour of sadness and joy you were evoking, Brother John of Fiesole, when your brush created the circle of the Elect, with Blessed Dominic, presented by an angel, advancing joyously to the foot of the throne of the Lamb?

The Feast of All Saints of the Order of Preachers,
November 12, 1960

Notes

1. Dominic was definitely the son of Juana de Aza, but it is possible that the eldest sons of Felix de Guzman were by a first marriage. In that case they would only be the half-brothers of the Saint.

2. Louis Lavelle, *Quatre Saints*, Paris, 1951.

3. Canticle of Canticles, 2:4.

4. Jordan of Saxony was both the earliest biographer of the saint and his successor as head of the Order. He knew the Father of the Preachers personally.

5. Epistle to the Galatians, 2:20.

6. Epistle to the Romans, 10:9,14.

7. Gospel of St. Matthew, 10.

8. Psalm 62.

9. Gospel of St. John, 17:3.

10. The two sources of morality and religion.

11. The word comes from the French "faide," private war, and was applied to those in southern France who refused to submit and fled to make war on the army of the Church; they were considered to be defenders of heretics (*Vicaire*, Vol. I, p. 280).

12. St. Thomas of Aquinas, *Summa Theologica*, IIa IIae Q. 182 a.I.

13. Gospel of St. John, 19:34.

Bibliography

H. D. Lacordaire, *Vie de saint Dominique,* Paris, 1922.

H. D. Laval, O.P., *Saint Dominique d'auprès l'œuvre de Fra Angelico,* Paris, 1952.

P. Mandonnet, O.P., *Saint Dominique, l'idée, l'homme et l'œuvre,* 2 vols., Paris, 1937; Eng. tr. 1944.

M. H. Vicaire, O.P., *Saint Dominique de Caleruega d'après les documents du xiii° siècle,* Paris, 1955.

M. H. Vicaire, O.P., *Histoire de saint Dominique,* 2 vols., Paris, 1957.

M. H. Vicaire, O.P. et L. Vonn Matt, *Saint Dominique, textes et légendes,* Paris, 1958.